LETTER TO A FALLEN AWAY CATHOLIC

CATHOLIC TREASURES
626 Montana Street
Monrovia, CA 91016

Originally Published by St. Peter Press
Fort Worth, Texas

Reprinted in 1994 by Catholic Treasures

Printed in the United States of America

ISBN 0-9620994-5-7

June 27, 1991
Feast of Our Lady of Perpetual Help

Dear Loved One,

More than likely, if you have managed to keep your sanity in today's sad and sinful world, you may have been scandalized even at what has been happening in the Catholic Church. At the present time, she seems to have fallen prey to all the snares of Satan set to trap not only the weakest of men but also the most brilliant of theologians.

How is it, you may well ask, that as a Catholic I can still profess allegiance to my Church? With the help of our dear Lord, and that of His most blessed Mother, I will try to explain. To begin with:

THE CATHOLIC CHURCH WAS FOUNDED DIRECTLY BY CHRIST

In the Old Testament the Jewish Tabernacle was the work of God – not man. It was God who drew up its plan, giving its exact dimensions, stipulating the materials to be used in its construction, describing its sacred furnishings and vessels for the service, and the vestments and ornaments for the priests who would minister therein. He gave it a suitable constitution, appointed its rulers, and defined the extent of their power. (See Book of Exodus, chapters 25 through 31, entire Book of Leviticus; Book of Numbers, chapters 1, 3 through 8, and 17 and 18.) So, since the Tabernacle of the *Old* Law (which was but a *shadow,* a *figure,* of the Church to come) was the work of God, surely the Church of the *New* Testament (the *substance,* the *reality)* must likewise be the work of God.

It is easily shown that it was Christ Himself, not His followers, not even His Apostles, who established the

Church: Christ declared His *intention* of founding a Church, by the institution of a living authority, when He said to Simon Peter: "Thou art Peter, and upon this rock I will build My Church, and the gates of hell shall not prevail against it" (Matt. 16:18). Now, if Christ intends personally to build His Church, it is not to be the work of man. Christ Himself will therefore give it all the necessary elements of a true social body, and, consequently, a ruling authority. And, that there might be no room for doubt, He added: "And I will give to thee the keys of the kingdom of heaven. Whatsoever thou shalt bind upon earth, it shall be bound also in heaven; and whatsoever thou shalt loose on earth, it shall be loosed also in heaven" (Matt. 16:19). This authority was *actually established* and the Church founded, when Our Lord after His resurrection said to Peter: "Feed My lambs; feed My sheep" (John 21:15,17). During His mortal life Christ Himself was the visible head of the infant Church, but after His Resurrection the office of visibly feeding the flock was to be discharged by another, to whom Christ gave the necessary authority and office. And as the followers of the law of Moses under the Old Testament formed one compact body, so too were the followers of Christ to be One Body: "One Lord, one faith, one baptism" (Ephesians 4:5). From the moment when first the Church, after the descent of the Holy Ghost, appeared before the world, we find a compact, fully organized society, with the apostles at its head. "They, therefore, who received his (Peter's) word were baptized; and there were added in that day about three thousand souls. And they were persevering in the doctrine of the apostles, and in the communication of the breaking of bread, and in prayers" (Acts of the Apostles, 2:41,42).

It was by the preaching of the apostles, it is true, that the faithful were gained for the Church; but it was not the apostles who devised the plan of this body, made baptism the condition of membership, appointed the first supreme head, and invested him with authority. It was Christ Himself who did all this, and by so doing founded the Church. A "church of the future" is, therefore, no less absurd than a Christian religion of the future, for the founder of the Christian religion was at the same time the immediate founder of the Church. Being outside the Church was considered by the early Church Fathers as being a non-Christian. "He is no Christian," says St. Cyprian (died 258), "who is not within the Church of Christ" (Ep. ad Antonian, 55, n.24).

CHRIST ESTABLISHED A VISIBLE CHURCH

In the New Testament we learn that Christ was visibly on earth but a very short time; that the term of His public teaching comprised only three years, which was occupied chiefly with the instruction of twelve men, who, under a chief, were to constitute His first representative corporate teaching body; they would be commissioned by the Son of God to "go forth and teach all nations" in His name (Matt. 28:18,19). They would have successors in office, since the Kingdom of Christ was not only to be world-wide, but would endure until the end of time: "of His Kingdom there shall be no end" (Luke 1:33). And though Jesus would return to Heaven, He would not be disassociated from His visible teaching body: "Behold, I am with you all days, even unto the consummation of the world" (Matt. 28:20). If men employ every means in their power for the perpetuation of their work, can we imagine that God left His great work to drift along unguided and unprotected? If the Bible teaches anything plainly it is the visibility of Christ's Church. It is composed of rulers and subjects: "Take heed to yourselves and to the whole flock in which the Holy Spirit has placed you as bishops to rule the Church of God, which He has purchased with His own blood" (Acts 20:28). Its members are admitted by a visible external rite (Baptism); they must hear, and obey: "He who hears you, hears Me; he who rejects you, rejects Me" (Luke 10:16). Christ compares His Church only to things visible: a "flock" (John 21:15-17), "a sheepfold" (John 10:16), a "city seated on a mountain" (Matt. 5:14), a "kingdom" (Matt. 13). He calls it "My

Church" (Matt. 16:18), (not *"Churches"*), *"The* Church" (Matt. 18:17). Fittingly, then, does this Kingdom of God upon earth merit the designation of St. Paul: "The Church of the living God" (1 Tim 3:15).

Pope Pius XI in an encyclical of January 6, 1928 on "Fostering True Religious Unity" states: "The Church thus wonderfully instituted could not cease to exist with the death of its Founder and of the Apostles, the pioneers of its propagation, for its mission was to lead all men to salvation without distinction of time or place. 'Going therefore, teach ye all nations' (Matt. 28:19). Nor could the Church ever lack the effective strength necessary for the continued accomplishment of its task, since Christ Himself is perpetually present with it, according to His promise: 'Behold, I am with you all days, even to the consummation of the world' (Matt. 28:20). Hence not only must the Church still exist today and continue always to exist, but it must ever be exactly the same as it was in the days of the Apostles. Otherwise we must say – which God forbid – that Christ has failed in His purpose, or that He erred when He asserted of His Church that the gates of hell should never prevail against it" (Matt. 16:18).

Forty-seven times the word "Church" is found in the Old Testament, and in each passage it means but *one* Church, *one* way of worshipping the Lord before the coming of Christ. That was the Jewish Church – the religion and the law of Moses established by God. From no other altars did God receive the sacrifice of prayer. They were all abominations to Him. "He who turneth away his ears from hearing the law, his prayer shall be an abomination" (Proverbs 28:9). In the New Testament, twenty-four times "the Church" is mentioned in the Acts of the Apostles, and you find but one Church mentioned. Sixty-eight times St. Paul speaks of "the Church" in his Epistles, everywhere meaning but the one Church of God. St. John speaks of "the Church at Ephesus," "at Smyra," "at Philadelphia," etc., but these were different dioceses. They all belonged to the Catholic Church under Peter.

CHRIST FOUNDED AN APOSTOLIC TEACHING BODY

After Christ appointed Apostles to carry on the work He had begun, He bade them go and teach all nations, baptizing those who would believe, and teaching them to observe whatsoever He had commanded. The Apostles were sent, not as mere messengers, but as ambassadors bearing Christ's authority and power, and teaching and ministering in His name and person; so that in hearing them men were hearing Him, and in despising them they were despising Him (Matt. 28:18-20; Luke 10:16). In order that they might carry out this commission, Christ promised them the Spirit of Truth. "I will ask the Father, and he shall give you another Paraclete, that he may abide with you forever. The spirit of truth, whom the world cannot receive, because it seeth him not, nor knoweth him: but you shall know him; because he shall abide with you, and shall be in you. He will teach you all things, and bring all things to your mind, whatsoever I shall have said to you" (John 14:16,17,26). Finally, He promised to be with them, not for a few years or a generation, but for all days, thereby indicating that the apostolic order should last beyond the lives of its present members, even to the end of time. "Behold I am with you all days, even to the consummation of the world" (Matt. 28:20). In thus constituting the apostolic body, Christ was in reality constituting His Church. The Church was no mere collection of individual believers, but a definite organization, which was to be the pillar and ground of truth: "I write these things to thee hoping to come to thee shortly, but in order that thou mayest know, if I am delayed, how to conduct thyself in *the house of God*, which is *the Church of the living God, the pillar and mainstay of the truth*" (1 Tim. 3:14,15). It was to be founded on a rock. "Thou art Peter; and upon this rock I will build My Church" (Matt. 16:18). The Church taken as a whole comprises teachers and believers, but its essential constitution lies in the existence of a teaching authority, guaranteed by Christ to be *infallible*. "Thou art Peter; and upon this rock I will build My Church, *and the gates of hell shall not prevail against it*" (Matt. 16:18).

Such was the original constitution of the Church; and as the Church was to last for all ages, it is natural to suppose that it should always continue to exist according to its original constitution – that is to say, as an apostolic teaching body. There are no signs that this organization was a temporary expedient, to die out after a few years and leave a totally different system in its place. He did not say to His Apostles: "Lo! I am with you even to the end of your *lives;*" but "Lo! I am with you all days, *even to the consummation of the world.*" So that those to whom he addressed himself were to live to the end of the world! What does this mean, but that the Apostles were to have successors, in whom their rights were to be perpetuated? Successors whom Jesus would ever assist by His presence and uphold by His power. The work founded by a *God*, out of His love for man, and at the price of His own precious Blood, must surely be imperishable!

PETER IS MADE CHIEF SHEPHERD OF CHRIST'S CHURCH; THE POPES SUCCEED PETER

The unique place of primacy Peter enjoyed among Jesus' apostles is especially evident from three Bible texts: Matt. 16:13-19; Luke 22:31 sqq., and John 21:15 sqq. The first passage tells us how our Savior changed Peter's name, by calling him "Kepha," the Aramaic word for "rock," which in Latin is "petros," from which derives the English "Peter." So "Peter" means "rock." (Formerly he had been known as "Simon.") By this symbolic act, the Lord meant to designate Peter as the foundation of the Church He intended to establish; Peter was to be the sign of stability, permanence, and unity. In this same passage, moreover, Peter is promised both the keys to heaven's Kingdom and the power to bind and to loose. Luke 22:24-32 is the text relating a controversy among the disciples. On this occasion Christ foretold that Peter was about to be put to the test by Satan: "Simon, Simon, behold Satan hath desired to have you, that he may sift you as wheat" (Luke 22:31). This test occurred, of course, at the hour of Calvary. "I tell you, Peter . . . that the cock shall not crow today, until you have three times denied that you know Me" (Luke 22:34). But the prayer of Christ, said for Peter in particular, would save him, so that he in turn might "confirm his brethren" in faith: "But I have prayed for thee, that thy faith fail not: and thou, being once converted, confirm thy brethren" (Luke 22:32). Again, therefore, Peter is the rock and bulwark of the faith. In John 21:15 sqq., Jesus fulfills His pledge to give Peter the keys of heaven. This is the beautiful passage in which Peter is made shepherd of Christ's universal flock. The Acts of the Apostles show us how Peter functioned in his role of chief shepherd. He is the primary spokesman for the apostles; even though we read of Peter's "standing with the Eleven," it is Peter who speaks. He is the principal preacher, the pacesetter for apostolic endeavor. Read, for example, Acts 1:15-26; 2:14-40; 3:1-26; 4:8; 5:1-11; 5:29; 8:14-17; etc. That Peter eventually went to Rome – clearly through the Spirit's guidance – is the testimony of St. Ignatius of Antioch (died 107), as well as several other ancient chroniclers. As early as the first century, too, Pope St. Clement I, a successor of Peter in Rome (even though St. John the Apostle still lived), demonstrates possession of full responsibility for the whole Church in a dispute involving the Corinthians. Tertullian and Hippolytus, both second-century witnesses, acknowledge Peter as the first in the succession of Bishops of Rome; St. Cyprian, in the third century, views the unity of the Church as originating from Peter. And from the second century on, the Bishop of Rome was asked for judgment in controversial ecclesial issues. (St. Peter and St. Paul's relics are in St. John Lateran Basilica in Rome.)

THE APOSTOLIC TEACHING BODY CONTINUES
TO THE PRESENT DAY

Passing through the ages, we find the same Apostolic system of teaching. Down to the sixteenth century, there existed in Christendom no other than this idea. The Bishops were looked upon as successors of the Apostles, and their unanimous teaching under the Pope was regarded as absolutely trustworthy – as truly representing the doctrine of Christ. The Church as a whole could not possibly fall into error – this was guaranteed by the promises of Christ: "The gates of hell shall not prevail against it" (Matt 16:18); and those who claimed scripture in support of new doctrines, and against the prevailing doctrine of the Church, were regarded as heretics and rebels against Christ, and against His authority delegated to the Church.

THE CHURCH CAME TO BE KNOWN AS
THE "CATHOLIC" CHURCH

The following is quoted from the book "Outlines of European History" by James Breasted and James Robinson, copyright 1914, which was used as a textbook at Classen Public High School in Oklahoma City in the 1930's. (So it is not a *Catholic* school history book.): "It was not until about the third century that Christians came to call their Church 'Catholic' (meaning 'universal'). The Catholic Church embraced all true believers in Christ, wherever they might be. To this one universal Church all must belong who hoped to be saved" (page 308). And then it quotes St. Cyprian (died 258) as follows: "Whoever separates himself from the Church is separated from the promises of the Church . . . He is an alien, he is profane, he is an enemy; he can no longer have God for his father who has not the Church for his mother. If any one could escape who was outside the Ark of Noah, so also may he escape who shall be outside the bounds of the Church." (Note: Breasted & Robinson's text errs, however, as to the date the Church came to be called "Catholic." St. Ignatius of Antioch (died 107) called the Church "Catholic" in his writings.)

So until the Sixteenth Century when Martin Luther broke away from the Catholic Church, the overwhelming majority of Christians were Roman Catholics.

THE PROTESTANT REBELLION

The Protestant rebellion continues to be in fact what its adherents call it today – a protest, and themselves Protest-ants, Protestants. A protest against what? *Against Christ's divinely constituted teaching authority in the world – His Church –* and the substitution of the Bible, interpreted by each individual, in its place. This ran counter to the almost unanimous conviction of Christendom for fifteen hundred years!

WHAT WERE THE CAUSES OF
THE PROTESTANT REBELLION?

First, there had been a gradual relaxation of discipline which had weakened authority and opened the way to many scandals and unpunished abuses in the ranks of the clergy. "At the close of the Middle Ages and dawn of the new era, the Papacy had been too eager in the pursuit of humanistic aims, had cultivated too exclusively merely human ideals of art and learning, and at the same time had become entangled in secular business and politics, and was altogether too worldly" (Grisar, "LUTHER", V. p. 427). Moreover, in Germany at this time the Bishops were mostly younger sons of princely or noble houses who were quite unfitted for their spiritual work. And as for the lower clergy, secular and religious, while many were zealous to diffuse religious knowledge by catechetical teaching, sermons, instructive publications and educational work in the elementary and middle schools, many others were quite neglectful of these sacred duties.

So there were abuses in the Church then, as there are today, and as there always will be. But "Blessed is he who shall not be scandalized in Me" (Luke 7:23). Christ did not guarantee His Church from *scandal*, but from *error*: "When He, the Spirit of truth, has come, He will teach you *all truth*" (John 16:13). There were scandals in the Church even while Jesus was with it. Judas was a thief, a traitor, and a suicide; Peter, the head, swore to a falsehood; James and John quarreled over supremacy; St. Peter and St. Paul were at variance over circumcision, and St. Paul excommunicated one of the faithful for unspeakable lust. The Church is made up of *men*, not *angels*. The triumph of the Church is not in being composed of sinless mortals, but in supplying sinful men with means to carry on the struggle against their vicious tendencies. But Jesus by His divine power granted that His Church, even though composed of weak and sinful men, would never teach *error*. The Church may have needed house cleaning in the sixteenth century, but the way to clean house is not to dynamite it. A child may have a very dirty face and yet be absolutely pure in body and soul. "I am black but beautiful," sings the Church to all men in the words of Solomon (Canticles 1:4); that is, although the Catholic Church, the very Body of Jesus Christ in time and space, may appear to the eyes of men as it were black and contemptible; but inwardly, that is, in its faith and morals, fair and beautiful in the eyes of God.

You cannot heal a diseased member of the body by cutting it off. Cut away a member of the body from the heart's blood, and it dies. The spark of life animating the body does not follow the severed member. The spark of life remains with the body, and the severed member begins to disintegrate and decay. This is precisely what happened to the followers of the revolution of the sixteenth century, as we shall soon see. "It follows that those who are divided in faith and in government cannot be living in one Body . . . and cannot be living the life of its one divine Spirit" (Encyclical of Pope Pius XII, "The Mystical Body of Christ").

No people can form by themselves a congregation or church, claiming that they follow the teachings of Christ. Christ did not say: "Thou art Luther and upon this rock I will build my Church" (or "Thou art Calvin, Knox, King Henry VIII," etc.). Numberless are the false churches. "Among you there will be lying teachers who will bring in destructive sects . . . and many will follow . . . " (2 Peter 2:1,2) . . . "and by pleasing speeches, and good words, seduce the hearts of the innocent" (Romans 16:18). "In the last times, some shall depart from the faith, giving heed to spirits of error and doctrines of devils . . . " (1 Tim. 4:1-2); "For there shall be a time, when they will not endure sound doctrine: but according to their own desires, they will heap to themselves teachers, having to themselves itching ears: and will turn away their hearing from the truth" (2 Tim. 4:3-4). "They received not the love of truth that they might be saved. Therefore God shall send them the operation of error, to believe lying" (2 Thess. 2:10-11). "There is a way that *seemeth* just to a man, but the ends thereof lead to death" (Proverbs 14:12).

CAUSE OF THE RAPID SPREAD AND ESTABLISHMENT OF PROTESTANTISM

How was it possible that the Revolution became so widespread in such a short period of time, and that whole nations gave up the faith of their forefathers? One cause which greatly contributed to the defection was that the civil rulers in Germany, Scandinavia, England, and elsewhere, took advantage of the disorder, seeing in the rebellion a coveted opportunity of gaining absolute control over the people and of confiscating the property of the Church; and they gave to the leaders of the rebellion a support without which the revolt everywhere would have failed utterly.

The traitorous political ambition of France helped set up Protestantism permanently in Europe. It was Cardinal Richelieu (1585-1642), Prime Minister and real ruler of France under Louis XIII, who, to ensure the political victory of France in Europe, took the side of the Protestant princes of Germany against the Catholic Emperor, Ferdinand II, at the most critical moment of the Thirty Years' War between the forces of Protestantism and Catholicism. Cardinal Richelieu hired the Protestant military genius, Gustavus Adolphus, for five tubs of gold, to enter the war against the Catholics. The defeat of Ferdinand made impossible his dream of a Europe united again as one family by the Faith, so close to realization but for the treachery of the French Cardinal.

Another cause was the popular unrest and love of novelty which characterized the sixteenth century, and the discontent and evil elements that are present at all times in every society. Furthermore, the recent invention of printing enabled the Protestants to circulate their teachings, thus confusing and deceiving the minds of simple folk.

THE CATHOLIC COUNTER-REFORMATION

Long before the Protestant revolt, all serious-minded Catholic men and women were convinced that a purification of the Church in her hierarchy and in her members was needed. Not the Catholic *religion*, as the Protestants maintained, but the *people* who professed that religion required reformation. "Men must be changed by religion," as one of the champions of true reform remarked, "not religion by men." Our Lord told us not to be scandalized when we see "cockle and wheat in His Church" (Matt. 13:24-30). But why blame the Church for bad

Catholics? All the bad Catholics in the world are not the Catholic Church. The Catholic Church holds the "deposit of Faith," spoken of by St. Paul (1 Tim. 6:20-21). The bad Catholics are bad not because of being Catholic, but because they neglect their Catholic duties and disgrace their exalted condition. "The Church is a *perfect* body, composed of *imperfect* men. This is the mystery of faith which is a stumbling block to those outside it" (St. Augustine).

So the first goal of the counter-reformation was the purification of the Church in her hierarchy, and in her members. The spread of error by Protestants, who attacked the Divine Constitution of the Church and her fundamental doctrines, also imposed upon the Catholic leaders the duty of setting forth in unmistakable and authoritative terms the true doctrine of Christianity contained in Scripture and Tradition. For this purpose, an ecumenical council was convened (The Council of Trent, the Nineteenth Council of the Church) in the year 1545. The Council set up a vast program to restore religious discipline, revive Faith, and check the spread of Protestantism by defining dogmatically the doctrines under attack and censuring the errors of the rebellion.

There is no better proof for the divine origin and guidance of the Church than the fact that she not only survived the great Protestant Revolt of the Sixteenth Century, but emerged from the conflict rejuvenated and prepared to meet new ones.

With regard to the teachings of the "reformers":

WHICH WAS APPOINTED BY CHRIST TO TEACH MANKIND THE TRUE RELIGION – THE CHURCH OR THE BIBLE?

When our Divine Saviour sent His Apostles throughout the world to preach the Gospel to every creature, He laid down the conditions of salvation thus: "He who believeth and is baptized shall be saved, but he who believeth not shall be condemned" (Mark 16:16). Here, then, our Blessed Lord laid down two absolute and universal conditions – Faith and Baptism. What is this Divine Faith which we must have in order to be saved? It is to believe, *upon the authority of God,* "all things whatsoever" (Matt: 28:20) He has revealed. Therefore if a man would be saved he must profess the *true* Religion. Now if God commands me under pain of damnation to believe what He has taught, He is bound to give me the means to know what He has taught. What is this means?" "The Bible," say the Protestants. But we Catholics say, "No, not the Bible, but the Church of God." For if God had intended that man should learn his religion from the Bible, surely God would have given that book to man. But He did not do so. Christ sent His apostles throughout the earth and said: "Go ye therefore, and teach all nations, baptizing them in the name of the Father, and of the Son, and of the Holy Ghost, teaching them to observe all things whatsoever I have commanded you" (Matt. 28:19,20). Christ did not say, sit down and write Bibles, and then let every man read and judge for himself. Since the sixteenth century we have seen the result of such thinking in the founding of hundreds of religions by men, all quarreling with one another about the interpretation of the Bible. Jesus never wrote a line of scripture nor did He command His Apostles to do so, except when He directed St. John to write the Apocalypse (Book of Revelations 1:11), but ordered them to "teach all nations" (Matt. 28:19). In Matt. 18:17, He does not say, "He who will not read the scriptures," but "he who will not hear the Church, let him be to thee as the heathen and the publican." The Apostles never circulated a single volume of scripture, but going forth, preached everywhere (Mark 16:20). It is true that our Lord said on one occasion, "Search the Scriptures for in them ye think ye have eternal life, and the same are they that give testimony of me" (John 5:39). This passage is quoted by Protestants in favor of private interpretation but proves nothing of the kind. Our Saviour speaks here only of the *Old* Testament, because the New Testament was not yet written. He addressed, not the Apostles, but the Pharisees, and reproaches them for not admitting His Divinity, clearly known and shown by the prophets of the Old Testament.

The Church established by Christ existed about 65 years before St. John wrote the last book of the Bible. During these years how did the people know what they had to do to save their souls? Was it from the Bible they learned it? No, because the Bible as such was not yet composed. They knew it precisely as we know it, from the teaching of the Church of God. The New Testament writings were not gathered together and declared to be divinely inspired until late in the fourth century. Moreover, these witnesses were Catholics, and accepted the Scriptures as divinely inspired because their Church declared them to be so. Protestants hold that the writings, known as the Sacred Scriptures, are inspired. But it is on the Catholic Church's word that they hold this truth! They take for granted that followers of the Catholic Church transcribed and translated the original writings without making any errors, that they never altered a line, that they preserved them until the sixteenth century in their original purity and integrity. Unless they grant all this, they cannot logically appeal to the Scriptures as divine authority. Thus Protestants are breaking away from their theory of "Nothing but the Bible" and basing their arguments on Tradition, or on the authority of the Catholic Church, which, on principle, they repudiate!

The Jewish religion existed before the Old Testament was written, just as the Christian Church existed before the New Testament was written. Peter converted three thousand before the first word of the New Testament was put on paper. Paul had converted hundreds of Romans, Corinthians, Galatians and Thessalonians before he wrote his epistles to those congregations; and all the Apostles were dead, and millions had died Catholic martyrs, before St. John wrote the last part of the New Testament. Until the end of the first century the "Word of God" could have been delivered only by *word of mouth*.

HOW THE APOSTLES REGARDED
THE NEW TESTAMENT

The Apostles seem to think it an important matter to leave us their recollections of Christ's life and character, but they make no pretense of giving us a complete written account of His teaching. They show no signs of regarding it as a duty to leave behind them full written particulars. St. John himself declares the impossibility of writing anything like an exhaustive account of all that Christ did (John 21:25). As far as we can gather, nearly all the Apostles were dead or dispersed before half the New Testament was written. None of the Apostles ever saw the Gospel of St. John, except the author himself. Only St. John lived long enough to have seen the whole series which made up the New Testament; but there is no evidence to show that he actually did see it. The only clear reference made by one Apostle to another Apostle's writings is that of St. Peter, who tells us how hard St. Paul's epistles were to understand, *and how some had wrested them to their own destruction* (2 Peter 3:16). Scripture was regarded as a *witness* to the Church's teaching, not as a sole and adequate Rule of Faith to be substituted in its place.

ST. PAUL USED THE SCRIPTURES

In the Acts of the Apostles 17:2, we are told that St. Paul reasoned with the Thessalonians on three Sabbath days "out of the Scriptures," and in verse 11, Paul says that Bereans "searched the Scriptures." Verse 2 implies that St. Paul used the Bible and verse 11 that the Bereans had it; but this was not the *New* Testament, for very little of it had been written at that time. Read verse 3, and it will be clear that he was appealing to the prophetic writings of the *Old* Testament, showing them that Christ was to suffer and to rise again. He didn't prove from the Scriptures that Christ had already suffered. The same applies to verse 11.

THE FIRST CHRISTIANS WERE NOT "BIBLE" CHRISTIANS

The various parts which now make up the New Testament were carefully treasured and read in the local churches where they had been received, but it was only by degrees that copies were spread to other places and the whole came to be circulated throughout Christendom. It was late in the fourth century before the present New Testament writings were gathered together into one book. It was this late in the Christian era before the Catholic Church declared which of the many doubtfully inspired writings scattered throughout the world were really inspired.

HOW THE EARLY CHRISTIANS RECEIVED THEIR FAITH

We find in the New Testament many references to Christian doctrine as derived from *oral* teaching. The Thessalonians are told to "hold fast the traditions which they had been taught, whether by *word* or by epistle" (2 Thess. 2:15). Timothy, who had been ordained Bishop of Ephesus by St. Paul is instructed to "Hold fast the form of sound words which he had *heard* from his teacher among many witnesses"; "to continue in the things learnt" (that is, "the gospel which was committed to his trust"), "knowing from whom he had learnt them," "and to commit the same to faithful men who shall be able to teach others" (1 Tim. 1-11; 4:11-16; 6:20; 2 Tim 1:6, 13; 2:2, 3:10, 14; 4:2, etc.) – all of which certainly stands in favor of the Catholic doctrine of apostolic authority in a line of successors, for an *oral* transmission of Faith, and against the Protestant idea of substituting the Bible as the sole and adequate guide to salvation. The Bishops were universally regarded as the authoritative successors to the Apostles responsible for the preservation of Christian doctrine. The New Testament was not completed until 65 years after Peter and Paul and most of the other Apostles were dead; many of their immediate successors had been martyred, and it is likely that the third or fourth successors of the several Apostles were converting souls without the Bible when St. John completed his writings. In fact, the whole Roman Empire was Christian, at least ten million people remained true to Christ and suffered a martyr's death, and the Church was enjoying her golden age, before anybody ever saw the New Testament bound up into one volume. For four centuries people received their faith only by *hearing* it preached in Catholic churches.

Most Protestants enter the Protestant religion through family ties or evangelistic services – not by Bible reading. Very few people are led to embrace this or that religion by "searching the Scriptures." Nine times out of ten, they enter a religion first, and do their Bible reading afterwards.

The Bible was not given from Heaven like the Ten Commandments were – as the Christian's sole rule of faith; and Christ did not write the New Testament; and the Apostles were not ordered to write it as a text book. *Tradition* is also a rule of faith; for "Faith cometh by *hearing*" (Rom 10:17).

IS SCRIPTURE INHERENTLY CLEAR?

Suppose: an Episcopal minister reads the Bible in a prayerful spirit and says it is clear and evident that there must be "bishops." The Presbyterian, a sincere and well-meaning man, deduces from the Bible that there should be no bishops, only "Presbyters." A number of religions hold that baptism by immersion is correct, while others approve of baptism by sprinkling. Next comes the Unitarian who calls them all a pack of idolators, worshipping a man for a God, and he quotes several texts from the Bible to prove it. So we have here a number of denominations understanding the Bible in different ways. What then, if we bring together 500 denominations all differing? One says there is no hell; another says there is. One says Christ is God; another says He is not, etc. Is baptism necessary for salvation? Must infants be baptized? Are good works necessary, or is faith alone sufficient? The correct answer to these questions is surely essential, but zealous Bible readers do not agree concerning them. Is anyone foolish enough to believe that the changeless and eternal Holy Spirit is directing those five hundred denominations, telling one Yes and another No; declaring a thing to be black and white, false and true, at the same time? If the Bible were intended as the guide and teacher of man, would St. Peter have declared that "In the scriptures are things hard to be understood, which the unlearned and unstable wrest to their own destruction" (2 Peter 3:16)?

On the contrary, the Bible itself declares that it contains many passages, the meaning of which is not clear. Read Acts 8:27-35; Luke 24:25-27; 2 Peter 3:16. Moreover, if the Bible is the Protestants' authority for everything, how is it that they cannot quote the Bible in favor of the "private judgment" theory? Not only can it not be found, but you will find this declaration in the holy book: "No prophecy of Scripture is made by private interpretation" (2 Peter 1:20). St. Paul warned Titus not to concede to anyone the right of private judgment (Titus 3:9-11).

PRIVATE INTERPRETATION HAS MADE OF THE BIBLE A BABEL OF CONFUSION

Individual opinions have divided Christianity, and occasioned more infidelity than anything else. W. E. Lecky, in "RATIONALISM IN EUROPE," Vol. II, p. 174, states: "It has been most abundantly proved that from Scripture, honest and able men have derived and do derive arguments in support of the most opposite opinions." And from "The London Times" of January 13, 1884: "England alone is reputed to contain some 700 sects, each of which proves a whole system of theology and morals from the *Bible.*"

THE MAJORITY OF CHRISTIANS DID NOT HAVE THE BIBLE BEFORE THE FIFTEENTH CENTURY

Not only was the Bible not the Christian's written Rule of Faith during the first four centuries, but it was not during the next thousand years, for the simple reason that there was no widespread use of paper to print on until the thirteenth century, and the moveable-type printing press itself was not invented until the year 1450, more than one thousand years after the true canon of the Bible (the collection of books which were considered inspired) was determined. Without the printing presses, it was impossible to distribute Bibles by hundreds of thousands. It required several years of work, distributed over many hours of the day, to produce *one* copy of the Bible. Every page had to be handmade, with pen upon parchment. Who copied these Bibles by hand? In most monasteries, from the early centuries, the daily occupation of many thousands of monks consisted in copying the scriptures for the benefit of the world. Some excellent specimens exist, one of them now being displayed at the Congressional Library, in Washington, D.C. A copy of the manuscript-Bible was usually placed on a large table in church, where the people who could read might have the benefit of it. Some Protestant Churches spread the falsehood that the Catholic Church chained the Bible so that people might not learn anything from it. That is an anti-Catholic fable. The thick cover of the Bible was chained to the table (or podium) so that no one might steal the valuable work. In those days a

Bible would have cost over $10,000.00. The Bible was displayed in the church, wide-open, precisely that it might be read. Not one in 50,000 had a Bible. Would our Divine Lord have left the world for 1500 years without that book if it were necessary to man's salvation? Most assuredly not. But suppose everyone had Bibles? What good will that book be, even today, to the one-half of the people of the world who cannot read?

THE FIRST PROTESTANTS TOOK OUR BIBLE, NOT WE THEIRS

The printing press was invented 65 years before Luther's revolt; and according to Hallam, a Protestant historian, the Catholic Bible was the first book ever printed. In 1877 there were exhibited hundreds of old Bibles, at South Kensington, England; it was called the "Caxton Exhibition," and among them were nine German editions of the Bible, printed in Germany before Luther was born; and there were more than one hundred editions of the Latin Bible, the very thing Luther is pretended to have "discovered." This disproves the popular lie about Luther finding the Bible at Erfurt in 1507. Many Protestant historians have repudiated this charge. To name a few: Dr. McGilfert in MARTIN LUTHER AND HIS WORK, page 273, says: "If Luther was ignorant of the Bible, it was his own fault. The notion that Bible reading was frowned upon by ecclesiastical authorities of that age is quite unfounded." And Dr. Preserve Smith in LIFE AND LETTERS OF MARTIN LUTHER, page 14, writes: "The book was a very common one, there having been no less than one hundred editions of the Latin Vulgate published before 1500, as well as a number of German translations." And Murzel in HISTORY OF GERMANY, Vol. II, p. 223, says: "Before the time of Luther, the Bible had already been translated and printed in both High and Low Dutch."

OUR LORD SET UP A SUPREME COURT

When the Constitution of the United States was written, its writers did not leave it to the people to interpret as they saw fit. They knew better than that. They set up a Supreme Court for that purpose. And do you think that the all-wise God would be less careful in a matter of even greater importance where the salvation of millions of immortal souls is at stake? Most assuredly not. He, too, set up a "Supreme Court," to guide and teach His people, and to interpret the law for them. In the Old Testament, God chose Moses to deliver His people, the Israelites, from the Egyptians, and to rule over them during their 40 years of wandering in the desert towards the promised land. In the Book of Numbers, Chap. 27, verses 12-23, as the time of his death approaches, Moses asks God to "provide a man that may be over this multitude and may lead them out, or bring them in: lest the people of the Lord be as sheep without a shepherd. And the Lord said to him: Take Josue – a man in whom is the Spirit – and put thy hand upon him . . . and thou shalt give him precepts in the sight of all . . . that all the congregation of the children of Israel may hear him . . . he and all the children of Israel with him, and the rest of the multitude shall go out and go in *at his word*." And in the Book of Deuteronomy, Moses was repeating and expounding to the Israelites the ordinances given on Mt. Sinai, with other precepts not expressed before. In Chapter 17, verses 8-12, he states: "If thou perceive that there be among you a hard and doubtful matter in judgment . . . and thou see that the words of the judges within thy gates do vary: arise, and *go up to the place, which the Lord thy God shall choose*. And thou shall come to the priests of the Levitical race, and to the judge that shall be at that time. And thou shalt ask of them. And they shall shew thee the truth of the judgment. And thou shalt do whatsoever they shall say, that preside in the place, which the Lord shall choose, and what they shall teach thee, according to His law. And thou shalt follow their sentence: *neither shalt thou decline to the right hand nor to the left hand*. But he that will be proud, and refuse to obey the commandment of the priest, who ministereth at that time to the Lord thy God (i.e., the high priest), and the decree of the judge: that man shall die . . ." And the footnote, Douay Bible, to this ordinance states: "Here we see what authority God was pleased to give to the church guides of the Old Testament, in deciding *without appeal*, all controversies relating to the law, *promising that they should not err therein*; and surely he has not done less for the church guides of the New Testament."

Christ set up that teaching organism called "the Church," with St. Peter and his successors as Chief Shepherd (that is, "high priest"), to be His official Custodian and interpreter under the New Law. And He promised to safeguard the Church from error. Read John 1:14; 14:6; 1 John 5:20; John 14:17; 15:26; 16:13; John 8:32; 17:17; 2 John 1:3. To that Church alone, and not to any *book* or *private individual* did He say "Teach ye all nations . . . I will be with you" (Matt. 28:20). And "He who will not hear *the Church*, let him be to thee as the heathen and the publican" (Matt. 18:17).

THE CATHOLIC CHURCH URGES ITS MEMBERS TO READ THE BIBLE

"At a time when a great number of bad books . . . are circulated among the unlearned . . . the faithful should be excited to the reading of the Bible; for this is the most abundant source which ought to be left open to every one to draw from it purity of morals and of doctrine" (Pope Pius VI, 1778). And Pope Leo XIII, elected in 1878, did much to promote the reading of the Holy Scriptures. He founded a congregation for the advancement of biblical studies; he addressed a letter to the whole Church on the subject of the reading and study of Holy Writ; and he granted special blessings to those who devoutly read the Holy Scriptures daily.

The Church authorities at the Synod of Oxford, in 1408, forbade the laity to read *unauthorized* versions of the Scriptures. In other words, she forbade them to accept as Scripture what really was not Scripture. For example, the Albigensians of the thirteenth century made a translation of the Bible which would square with their erroneous teachings. (See Hallam, MIDDLE AGES, Chapter IX). And Sir Thomas More says "Wycliffe took upon himself to translate the Bible anew. In this translation he purposely corrupted the holy text, maliciously planting in it such words as might, in the reader's ears, serve to prove such heresies as he 'went about to sow.' " (EVE OF THE REFORMATION, Gasquet, Chapter VIII). The Lollards changed the text still more, and made the Bible support the anarchy which they later preached throughout England.

HISTORY OF THE PROTESTANT ENGLISH BIBLE

"Tyndale's New Testament" was published under King Henry VIII; the "Bishop's Bible" in 1568; "The King James" or "Authorized Version" in 1611; "The Revised Version" in 1881. *Each of these was brought out because the previous one was found to contain errors.* (Read "History of the Reformation of the Church in England," by J. H. Blunt, Ch. I). Zwingli, writing to Luther, in commenting on his translation of the Bible into German, says: "Thou dost corrupt the word of God; thou art seen to be a manifest and common corrupter and perverter of the Holy Scriptures; how much are we ashamed of thee!" (Vol. II, DE SACRAMENTIS, p. 412). Here are some of his typical corruptions: "Wherefore, brethren," St. Peter commands us, "labor the more, that by good works you may make sure your vocation and election" (2 Peter 1:10); But Luther omitted the words "By good works." "We account a man to be justified by faith" (Romans 3:28). Luther added the word "alone." Calvin's translations of the Scriptures were equally faulty. A Protestant authority says: "Calvin makes the text of the gospel to leap up and down; he uses violence to the letter of the gospel, and besides this, adds to the text." (See Molinaeus' TRANSLATION OF THE NEW TESTAMENT, Part XI, p. 110). In his APOLOGY, Sec. 6, Mr. Burgess, a Protestant, says of the English Protestant version: "How shall I approve, under my hand, a translation which has many omissions, many additions; which sometimes obscureth, sometimes perverteth the sense, being sometimes senseless, sometimes contrary?"

So the prohibition of the Catholic Church against Bible-reading had reference to the reading of *faulty translations* of the Scriptures. Such faulty translations are not surprising, as the devil, too, quotes the Scriptures dishonestly: In Matthew 4:1-11, we read: "At that time, Jesus was led by the Spirit into the desert, to be tempted by the devil . . . Then the devil took Him up into the holy city, and set Him upon the pinnacle of the temple, and said to Him: if thou be the Son of God, cast thyself down. For it is written: That he hath given his angels charge over thee . . . " This we read in the 90th Psalm; but there the prophecy was not spoken of *Christ*, but of the *just man*; so the devil has quoted the Scriptures dishonestly. As Satan changes himself into an angel of light, and even from the Holy Scriptures prepares snares for Christians, so now he uses the testimonies of Scripture itself not to instruct, but to deceive.

THE CATHOLIC BIBLE CONTAINS MORE BOOKS THAN THE PROTESTANT BIBLE

Why? For the same reason that it contains any of the writings within its covers. As already explained, and no man in this world can refute it, the writings which the Protestants accept as inspired, they know to be so *only on the authority of the Catholic Church*. The Protestant Bible omits the following seven books from the Old Testament: Judith, Ecclesiasticus, Baruch, Tobias, Wisdom, and the two books of the Machabees. (Luther originally threw out 11 entire books!) These books are inspired Sacred Scripture, and for twenty centuries, from the compilation of the Old Testament canon by Esdras and Nehemias in 430 B.C., until the rebellion of the Protestants in the Sixteenth Century, they were accepted by the faithful as God's revelation to His people. They are still in the *Catholic* Bible.

Most of the Protestant and Catholic versions of the Bible have the same books in the New Testament. But the New Testament contains writings which were not written by the Apostles. Luke and Mark were not Apostles at all, and even Paul was not one of the original twelve. How could it possibly be proved, outside the Catholic Church's authority, that Mark's and Luke's writings were inspired? And how could one, rejecting this Church's authority, account for the omission of gospels written by St. Bartholomew and St. Thomas, and the acts of St. Andrew, who *were* apostles? Of these, several were regarded by certain of the Fathers as part of Scripture, and were publicly read in local Churches, while others in the second and third centuries classed them as doubtfully inspired. Likewise, the Epistle to the Hebrews, Revelations, James, Jude, 2nd Peter, and 2nd and 3rd John were at first called into question in some parts of the Church.

HOW THE CONTENTS OF THE NEW TESTAMENT WERE DETERMINED

So the collections of reputed inspired writings in different parts of Christendom in the second, third, and fourth centuries varied considerably, and it was at Church Councils at Hippo and Carthage (held between 393-419) that a list of authentic books was agreed upon. Pope Innocent I, and afterwards Pope Gelasius (A.D. 494), confirmed this list, and for the first time the New Testament was capable of being bound up into one book as we have it now. How was this question settled after so long a dispute? Purely and simply by an appeal to the traditions existing in local churches where each document had been preserved, and by the authoritative verdict of the Church, judging according to those traditions. Hence, the reliability of the Bible depends wholly on the authority of the *Roman Catholic Church*! Protestants, in accepting the New Testament as it stands, are acknowledging the authority of the Catholic Church in the fourth and fifth centuries, and some of them have candidly admitted this in writing. (See preface to Revised Version of Protestant Bible.)

HOW OLD ARE THE PROTESTANT CHURCHES?

The Lutheran Church was founded in the year 1517 by Martin Luther, a former priest of the Roman Catholic Church.

The Church of England (Anglicanism) was founded by King Henry VIII in 1534 when he threw off the authority of the Pope and proclaimed himself the head of the Church in England, because the Pope refused to declare invalid his marriage with Queen Catherine.

The Presbyterian denomination was begun in 1560 by John Knox who was dissatisfied with Anglicanism.

The Episcopalian denomination was begun in 1784 by Samuel Seabury who was dissatisfied with Presbyterianism.

The Baptist church was launched by John Smyth in Amsterdam, Holland in the year 1606.

The Methodist church was launched by John and Charles Wesley in England in 1744.

The Unitarians were founded by Theophilus Lindley in London, in 1774.

The Jehovah's Witness Church was developed in 1872 by Charles Russell.

The founder of The Salvation Army is William Booth, who quit the Anglicans, and then the Methodists, and set up his own version of Christianity in 1787. His own son, Ballinger, quit The Salvation Army and did the same for himself in 1896.

Mrs. Mary Baker Eddy began the Christian Scientist religion in 1879, basing it upon an outright denial of Original Sin and its effects.

The Mormon church, the Seventh-Day Adventists, the Church of Christ, The Church of the Nazarene, or any of the various Pentecostal Churches, etc. are also among the hundreds of new churches founded by *men* within the past few generations.

The Roman Catholic Church was founded by God-made-man, Jesus Christ, in the year 33 A.D. He said: "Thou art Peter, and upon this rock I will build My Church, and the gates of hell shall not prevail against it . . . Feed my lambs; feed My sheep" (Matt. 16:18,19; John 21:15,17). He also said: "He who is not with Me is against Me, and he who gathers not with me scatters" (Matt. 12:30).

MARTIN LUTHER

The Protestant Revolution was begun by Martin Luther, a Catholic priest, who, led astray by private judgment, set himself against the Faith held for 1500 years. He decided that all Christians before him had been in error. *Is it possible to believe that Jesus founded a Church to mislead the world, and then after 1500 years approved of over 500 contradictory churches founded by men?* But, you may say, the Protestant Church is the Church of Christ, purified of error, and only this purified form dates from Luther. I answer that you must choose between Luther and Christ. Jesus said His Church would never teach error (John 14:26); Luther says it did teach error. If Luther is right, Christ is wrong; if Christ is right, Luther and all his followers are wrong.

Luther's chief errors are contained in the following propositions: (1) There is no supreme teaching power in the Church. (2) The temporal sovereign has supreme power in matters ecclesiastical. (3) There are no priests. (4) All that is to be believed is in the Bible. (5) Each one may interpret Holy Scripture as he likes. (6) Faith alone saves, good works are superfluous. (7) Man lost his free will by original sin. (8) There are no saints, no Christian sacrifice, no sacrament of confession, no purgatory.

Following are some significant excerpts from Luther's writings and lectures, as compared with the teachings of our Lord Jesus Christ. (Taken from the book CHRIST VS. LUTHER, edited by R. A. Short, copyright 1953 by the Bellarmine Publishing Company, Mound, Minn.)

– On Sin –

Christ: "Now the works of the flesh are manifest, which are fornication . . . murder . . . and suchlike. And concerning these I warn you, they who do such things will not attain the Kingdom of God" (Galatians 5:19-21).

Luther: "Sin boldly but believe more boldly. Let your faith be greater than your sin . . . Sin will not destroy us in the reign of the Lamb, although we were to commit fornication a thousand times in one day" (Letter to Melanchton, August 1, 1521, Audin p. 178).

Christ: "And do not be drunk with wine, for in that is debauchery" (Eph. 5:18). "Keep thyself chaste" (I Tim. 5:22).

Luther: "Why do I sit soaked in wine? . . . To be continent and chaste is not in me" (Luther's diary).

– On Good Works –

Christat: "What will it profit, my brethren, if a man says he has faith, but does not have works?" "As the body without the spirit is dead, so faith without works is dead also" (James 2:14,26).
Luther: "He that says the Gospel requires works for salvation, I say, flat and plain, is a liar" (Table Talk, Weimer Edition, II, p. 137).

– On Truth –

Christat: "Do not be liars against the truth. This is not the wisdom that descends from above. It is earthly, sensual, devilish" (James 3:14-15). "Do not lie to one another" (Col. 3:9). "The Lord hateth . . . a lying tongue . . . a deceitful witness that uttereth lies . . . " (Proverbs 6:16-17). "A thief is worse than a liar, but both of them shall inherit destruction" (Ecclus. 20:27).
Luther: "To lie in case of necessity, or for convenience, or in excuse, would not offend God, who is ready to take such lies on Himself" (Eisenrach Conference, July 17, 1540).

– On Marriage –

Christat: "Whosoever shall put away his wife and marry another, committeth adultery against her. And if the wife shall put away her husband, and be married to another, she committeth adultery" (Mark 10:11-12).
Luther: "As to divorce, it is still a moot question whether it is allowable. For my part, I prefer bigamy" (DeWette, Vol. 2, p. 459).

– On Free Will –

Christat: "Woe to that man by whom the Son of Man is betrayed! It were better for that man if he had not been born" (Matt. 26:24). "Let no man say when he is tempted, that he is tempted by God; for God is no tempter to evil" (James 1:13).

<u>Luther</u>: "Judas' will was the work of God; God by His almighty power moved his will as He does all that is in this world" (De Servo Arbitro – Against man's free will). Accosted on all sides by charges of heresy, even by many of his former associates in the Protestant movement, Luther found refuge in this, the strangest of all his beliefs. No man is accountable for his actions, Luther taught, no matter how evil. Not even Judas!

Such are the teachings of the first so-called "reformer" of Christ's Church! If Luther was a man divinely inspired or called in an extraordinary manner, why did God permit him to fall into so many absurdities in points of doctrine?

"Luther finally brought himself to indulge the pleasing delusion that the Catholic Church was the detestable kingdom of Antichrist . . . that he himself was John the Evangelist . . . " (From the book LUTHER, P. 65).

So you see the heresies, divisions, confusion, etc. resulting from the private interpretation of the Scriptures. *Unless there is a church in the world, from the days of our Lord, which declares unmistakably (infallibly) who Jesus is, and what He taught, He might just as well have revealed nothing*!

CHRIST DID ESTABLISH SUCH A CHURCH, AND IT IS THE ROMAN CATHOLIC CHURCH

When Christ left us and ascended into Heaven, He gave His powers to the Church He had founded: "All power has been given Me by My Father; go then" (in virtue of this power that I delegate to you) "teach all nations to keep My commandments. He who hears you, hears Me; he who despises you, despises Me" (Matt. 28:18-20; Luke 10:16). So the Church is invested with the authority of Jesus Christ; she speaks and commands in Our Lord's name. The difference between Protestants and Catholics lies in the attitude of dependance on and of obedience to the living authority of the Church which teaches and governs in the name of Christ. The Catholic accepts the Church's doctrines, and regulates his conduct according to those doctrines, because he hears in the Church, and her head the Sovereign Pontiff, the voice of Christ. The Protestant admits a certain truth because he "discovers" it, or imagines himself to do so, by his personal lights. Claiming the right of private interpretation (despite 2 Peter 1:20; 3:16) and reading the Bible according to his reason alone, he takes or leaves what he will. Each one then, keeping his faculty of choosing, becomes his own sovereign pontiff. The Protestant *admits*; the Catholic *believes*. As soon as the Church speaks, the Catholic submits in all obedience as to Christ Himself. St. Isidore (Archbishop, Doctor, and Saint) stated: "We, as Catholics are not permitted to believe anything of our own will, nor to choose what someone has believed of his. We have God's apostles as authorities, *who did not themselves of their own wills choose anything of what they wanted to believe*, but faithfully transmitted to the nations, the teachings of Christ." In the Old Testament God spoke to the Israelites from the midst of the two Cherubim atop the Ark of the Covenant: "There will I give orders, and will speak to thee over the propitiatory, and from the midst of the two Cherubims, which shall be upon the Ark of the Testimony, all things which I will command the children of Israel . . . " (Exodus 25:22). Today He speaks to us through the Catholic Church. She, alone, speaks with His Voice.

THE CATHOLIC CHURCH CLAIMS TO BE INFALLIBLE IN HER TEACHINGS

In order to keep His Church in the truth, Christ sent His Spirit – the Spirit of Truth (John 14:17). "When the Spirit of truth is come, He will teach you all truth" (John 16:13); "He will teach you all things, and bring all things to your mind, whatsoever I shall have said to you" (John 14:26). (So nothing of what the divine Word spoke to men is to be lost)! "He will abide with you forever; and He shall be in you" (John 14:16,17). It is by the Holy Spirit, then, that the Church is ever to possess the truth, and nothing can rob her of it; for this Spirit, who is sent by the Father and the Son, will abide unceasingly *with* and *in* her.

The Holy Spirit is the principle of the Church's life. He makes Himself responsible for her words, just as *our spirit* is responsible for what our *tongue* utters. Hence it is that the Church, by her union with the Holy Spirit, is so identified with truth, that the apostle did not hesitate to call her "the pillar and ground of the truth" (1 Tim. 3:14-15). Consequently, the Church *has* to be infallible in her teaching; for how can she be deceived herself, or deceive others, seeing it is the Spirit of Truth who guides her in all things and speaks by her mouth? He is her soul; and when the tongue speaks, the soul is responsible.

The man who does not acknowledge the Church to be infallible, should, if he be consistent, admit that the Son of God has not been able to fulfil His promise, and that the Spirit of truth is a Spirit of error. He thought he was but denying a prerogative to the Church, whereas, in reality, he has refused to believe *God Himself*. It is this that constitutes the sin of heresy. Want of due reflection may hide the awful conclusion; but the conclusion is strictly implied in his principle.

In the year 52, all the Apostles came together at Jerusalem, under St. Peter, to talk over the affairs of the Church. This was the first Council of the Church, and the story of it is told in the Acts of the Apostles, Chapter 15. The Councils are an Apostolic institution, and the Apostles, when they instituted them, acted under the commission they received from Christ; otherwise they could not have published the decisions of their Council with the words, "It seemed good to the Holy Ghost and to us" (Acts 15:28).

The Apostles spoke with unerring authority, and their words were received not as human opinions, but as Divine Truths. "When you have received from us the word of God, you received it not as the word of *men,* but as the word of *God"* (1 Thess. 2:13).

THE POPE IS NOT INFALLIBLE IN ALL HIS ACTS

The President of the United States does not always act as President. No one would attribute presidential authority to his views on hunting, or yachting, or on drama. Even when he presides over a White House function he is not always using his presidential prerogatives. No one would attach the full authority of the United States Government to the remarks he makes to a deputation of Presbyterians, Jews, or Catholics. Even when speaking in a cabinet meeting, or making his official speech at the opening of Congress, he does not intend to throw the full weight of his authority into his utterances. It is only when signing an Act of Congress or a treaty with some foreign nation, that the full and highest exercise of his presidency comes into play. Then, and then alone, does he act as ruler of the Country, committing the Government to the deed, and binding the whole nation. As it is with the President of the United States, so it is with the Pope. In his private acts as a Christian or Bishop, or in his jurisdiction of the government of the Church, he might make a mistake or fail in prudence.

Therefore, the Bishop of Rome, the Pope, *can* make a mistake – unless he is speaking under certain conditions. These conditions are: (1) when he is speaking "ex cathedra" (from the Chair of Peter); and (2) manifests his intention of defining a doctrine (3) of faith or morals (4) officially binding the whole Church. At such a time the Pope's teaching is infallible; that is, at such a time he is assisted, watched over, by the Holy Spirit so that he does not use his authority and his knowledge to mislead the

Church. The Pope is not inspired; he receives no private revelations; he does not carry in his mind the whole of Christ's teaching as a miraculous treasure on which to draw at will. He has learned the faith as we learned it, from his catechism and from his study of theology. If he wishes to know the two sides of a dispute he must examine it as we must. When preparing to make a definition in his office of supreme teacher, he first gives the matter to his theologians. They examine the sources of the doctrine in Holy Scripture and Tradition. These sources are what is called "The Deposit of Faith." The "Deposit of Faith" preserved by the Catholic Church includes: (1) Doctrines clearly taught in the Bible; (2) Doctrines obscurely taught in the Bible, and requiring the authority of the Church to decide their true interpretation; (3) Doctrines not mentioned in the Bible at all, for example: the abrogation of the Jewish Sabbath, with the obligation of observing Sunday instead; the practice of eating meat with blood, which was forbidden for a time by the Apostles (Acts 15:20). The "Deposit of Faith" is the body of truth divinely proclaimed by Our Lord through His Apostles for our belief. These truths of Revelation were complete at the death of the last Apostle – St. John – who died in the year 99 A.D. These truths, which we must believe in order to be Catholics, were all given to us by that time. The dogmas (doctrines) of the Church never can suffer change. They are today precisely what they were at the beginning of the Church. There are no new doctrines, and there can be no modification of old ones. "The doctrine of faith which God revealed," says Vatican Council I (1869-1870), "is proposed, not as a mere philosophical discovery to be elaborated by human minds, but as *the Divine Deposit delivered by Christ to His spouse* (the Church) to be by her faithfully guarded and infallibly declared."

Whenever a heretic challenged some revealed truth of the Faith, it became necessary for the Pope, either alone or together with his Bishops in Council, to re-express in more exact language the doctrine under attack, *so that never again could there be any doubt about its meaning.* This was done by definition. This does not mean that a new dogma is ever added to the Faith, or that something is added to an old dogma. It means merely that doubt or confusion has been cast on a doctrine, and it has become necessary for the Pope to remove the doubt and confusion. The theologians will find the doctrine stated either explicitly or implicitly in the "Deposit of Faith," and it is the truth either way. A doctrine is *explicitly* expressed when it is brought out definitely in words, openly, plainly. A dogma is *implicitly* expressed when it is hinted at but not specifically stated.

So a definition of a doctrine is the more precise expression of the doctrine. Its purpose is to *clarify*. In other words, a definition is the last word on the subject. Papal definition precludes any further interpretation of a dogma. The Church has taught from its beginning that no matter how much a doctrine may be developed or meditated upon, never, never can its meaning in any way be changed. Pope Leo XIII in his Encyclical "Testem Benevolentiae" of January 22, 1899 stated: " . . . That sense of the sacred dogmas is to be faithfully kept which Holy Mother Church has once declared, and is not to be departed from under the specious pretext of a more profound understanding" (Const. de Fid. cath. c. iv.).

A formula is generally used when a doctrine on faith or morals is defined ex cathedra, such as: "The most Holy Roman Church firmly believes, professes and preaches. . . ," or "We declare, say, define, and pronounce. . ." This lays great emphasis upon the statement, as did our Lord's "Amen, amen I say to you. . ." Note the formula in the proclamation of the dogma of the Immaculate Conception: " . . . We declare, pronounce and define: the doctrine that maintains that the most Blessed Virgin Mary in the first instant of her conception . . . was preserved free from all stain of original sin . . . is a doctrine revealed by God and therefore must be firmly and constantly held by all the faithful . . . "

So, when the Pope comes finally to the act of definition – when, acting in his highest official capacity of teacher of the Universal Church, he defines a point of faith or morals, with the intent of binding the whole Church – then we believe, by virtue of Christ's promise, that the decision will be infallibly right.

The Pope is also infallible when he teaches the Church as head of all his Bishops in assembly (in Council). An Ecumenical or General Council is a Council summoned by the Pope. It is made up of Bishops of the whole world, and other high ranking prelates with a right to vote. Its decrees are not binding until approved by the Pope. Only its *doctrinal* decrees, when they are confirmed by the Pope, are infallible. (Vatican Council II was a *Pastoral* Council, not a Doctrinal Council, and thus, none of its decrees are in themselves infallible.) The Pope is also infallible when he acts singly, by himself, as the head of the Church – provided he makes it clear that he is speaking ex cathedra (from the Chair of Peter) in defining a dogma, of faith or morals, for the whole Church.

A Papal Encyclical or Allocution is not an instrument of *definition*. These documents may speak on the subject of a doctrine of the Church though; and, if so, what is expounded by the Pope in them does demand consent *if they reiterate Catholic doctrine*. (The value of Tradition is such that even the Encyclicals and other documents of the ordinary teaching of the Sovereign Pontiff are infallible *only when the teachings are confirmed by Tradition*.) There actually have been times in the history of the Church when the Pope, speaking unthinkingly and from his first hasty judgment (and not ex cathedra), has erred in a matter of doctrine. Pope John XXII made just such a mistake, and it was the people who discovered it, and called it to his attention. He investigated the matter, acknowledged his misconception, and corrected his statement. The Holy Ghost will not allow error in Faith or morals to be officially taught by the Church!

The Apostles were the original teachers of the pure doctrine of Jesus Christ. Their teachings were regarded as holy and unchangeable. They insisted on unity of Faith among the Christians, and on a full acceptance of every single dogma of the Faith. St. James in his Epistle, Chapter 2, Verse 10, states: "And whosoever shall keep the whole law, but offend in *one point,* is become guilty of *all."* And the footnote to this verse, Catholic Douay Bible, states: "That is, he becomes a transgressor of the law in such a manner, that the observing of all other points will not avail him to salvation; *for he despises the lawgiver,* and breaks through the great and general commandment of charity, even by one mortal sin. For all the precepts of the law are to be considered as one total and entire law, and as it were a chain of precepts, where, by breaking one link of this chain, the whole chain is broken, or the integrity of the law consisting of a collection of precepts. A sinner, therefore, by a grievous offence against any one precept, incurs eternal punishment."

Thus, anyone who refused to accept all the doctrines of the Church, was immediately excommunicated, called a heretic, and shunned by the faithful. "A man that is a heretic, after the first and second admonition, avoid: knowing that he that is such a one is subverted and sinneth, being condemned by his own judgment" (Titus 3:10-11).

A doctrine or a dogma of the Church, then, is a truth which has been revealed by God, and must be believed by all. One cannot choose one, discard another. To say that we approve some, and disapprove others, *is to presume to stand in judgment of the truths of God.*

HERESIES IN THE CHURCH

"Heresies have often arisen and still arise because of this, that disgruntled minds will quarrel, or disloyal trouble-makers will not keep the unity. But these things the Lord allows and endures, leaving man's freedom unimpaired, so that when our minds and hearts are tested by the touchstone of truth, the unswerving faith of those who are approved may appear in the clearest light. This is foretold by the Holy Spirit through the Apostle Paul when he says: 'There must be also heresies, that those approved may be manifest among you' (1 Cor. 11:19). Thus are the faithful proved, thus the faithless discovered; thus too even before the day of judgment, already here below, the souls of the just and unjust are distinguished, and the wheat is separated from the chaff" (St. Cyprian, Bishop of Carthage, 249-258, on "The Unity of the Catholic Church" from the book ANCIENT CHRISTIAN WRITERS, page 52).

"They went out from us but they were not of us. For if they had been of us, they would no doubt have remained with us . . . " (1 John 2:19).

"When" says St. Cyprian "the devil saw that the worship of idols was abolished, and the heathen temples emptied (after Christianity was flourishing), he thought of a new poison, and led men into error under cover of the Christian religion and the poison of false doctrine . . . " The subtle and wicked doctrine which opened the way for the succession of heresies which were soon to harass the Church in the East, was an attack on the Divinity of Our Lord, Jesus Christ. Arius, a priest of Alexandria, Egypt in the Fourth Century, declared that the second person of the Holy Trinity was not equal with the Father; which was to say, that the nature which Jesus possessed in the Godhead from all eternity was not divine: Christ was not God! Arianism spread like wildfire in spite of its condemnation by the Council of Nicea in 325. Cardinal Newman conservatively estimated that *eighty per cent* of the Bishops of the Catholic Church followed Arius into heresy. "The whole world groaned to find itself Arian," St. Jerome complained. Lucifer did not stop there. The plan unfolds with startling clarity in the heresies which immediately follow. Around the year 360, Macedonius, then Bishop of

40

Constantinople, denied the Divinity of the Holy Ghost. In 428, Nestorius, also Bishop of Constantinople, threw all subterfuge to the winds and declared openly that Mary was not the Mother of God. He did this by making Jesus out to be not one person but two persons! In 451 the Abbot Eutyches, of Constantinople, said that Christ had only one nature – the divine – instead of two – the divine and the human; thus making Jesus out to be not true man, and therefore, not the fruit of Mary's womb. Christendom rocked upon its foundations. It was torn and bleeding and wounded. But Lucifer, in the end, had raged in vain. For, as is always God's way in times of great stress in His Church, God raised up strong men and holy women who, fortified by grace, came to her defence. These were the spiritual children of Heaven's Queen, the Blessed Virgin Mary, who, when the interests of her Divine Son and His Mystical Body are imperiled, is ever terrible as an army set in battle array. And so a veritable host of champions of the Faith arose – men who were so carried away with the love of God and ardor for the Faith that they became saints: The renowned St. Athanasius, who did battle against Arius (With so many of the faithful having followed Arius into heresy, it seemed for a time that it was "Athanasius against the world"); St. Gregory Nazianzen, who valiantly waged war against Macedonius; St. Cyril of Alexandria, who, with inimitable courage, held out against Nestorius; and Pope St. Leo the Great, who, in the name of Peter, vanquished Eutyches. Pope Leo XIII in his Encyclical Letter on the "Unity of the Church" (June, 1896), stated: "The Church . . . regards as rebels and expelled from the ranks of her children all who hold beliefs on any point of doctrine different from her own. The Arians and the Eutychians certainly did not reject all Catholic Doctrine: they abandoned only a certain portion of it. Still, who does not know that they were declared heretics and banished from the bosom of the Church? In like manner were condemned all authors of heretical tenets who followed them in subsequent ages. There can be nothing more dangerous, than those heretics who admit nearly the whole cycle of doctrine, and yet *by one word*, as with a drop of poison, infect the real and simple faith taught by our Lord and handed down by Apostolic tradition." St. Augustine notes that other heresies may spring up, to a single one of which, should anyone give his assent, he is by that very fact cut off from Catholic unity; and St. Thomas Aquinas asserts that anyone who denies a single article of faith is by that very fact excommunicated.

"Now I recall to your minds, brethren, the gospel that I preached to you, which also you received, wherein also you stand, through which also you are saved, *if you hold it fast, as I preached it to you* . . . " (1 Cor. 15:1-2).

MOST OF THE GREAT HERESIES WERE STARTED BY MEN WHO HELD HIGH ECCLESIASTICAL POSITIONS

Arius was a priest, Nestorius a patriarch, Eutyches an abbot, Luther a monk (a priest in a monastic order), and Jansenius a bishop. They are like coiners of false money who put into circulation worthless metal in the place of the pure gold of truth. They are murderers of souls, for they take men away from the road that leads to eternal life, and tempt them into that which leads to eternal death. It is of them that our Lord says: "Woe to them by whom scandals come" (Matt. 18:7), and again, "Beware of false prophets, who come to you in the clothing of sheep, but inwardly they are ravening wolves" (Matt. 7:15).

Those Catholics who place *obedience* above *doctrine* and follow their Bishops and Priests into heresy disobey God, cut themselves off from the Church, and forfeit their right to the kingdom of Heaven. The Church holds that this is misguided and sinful obedience. The people should withstand false doctrines. What is more, they should admonish the heretical shepherds. Blind obedience leads to Hell: "If the blind lead the blind, *both* fall into the pit" (Matt. 15:14).

What is now called the Greek Orthodox Church was once a part of the Holy Roman Catholic Church, but the people of the East continued to be obedient to their bishops even when those bishops had shown themselves to be heretical and had broken with the successor of St. Peter.

How, it will be asked, could the people possibly know the truth under the circumstances, if their bishops and priests did not know it? The answer is that their bishops and priests *did* know it – just as they know it today – but they deliberately chose heresy over truth for the material advantages it would bring them. Their object was not to spread the faith in its purity, but to satisfy their own evil inclinations, their pride, their sensual desires, or their love of money or popularity. Their religious teaching was only a cloak for their vices. *In any and all events they did not truly love Jesus Christ, for Jesus says, "He who loves Me keeps My words"* (John 14:15).

But how could the people know that they should not trust their shepherds? Was it not touching that they should obey? The answer is "No"! The lukewarm, indifferent, and those who were lazy in their faith did not recognize heresy, even when it affected them and their eternal destiny. They did not *deserve* to know, because they did not *desire* to know. In days like ours, when error is so pretentious and aggressive, every one needs to be completely armed with sound knowledge, since an important part of the fray must be borne by the laity, and woe to them if they are not well prepared. *"Therefore My people are led away captive because they had not knowledge"* (Is. 5:13).

THE ORDER OF OBEDIENCE

St. Ignatius Loyola, in the first of six volumes of the Spanish editions of his letters to the Society of Jesus in Portugal, says: "Obedience is not blind, inasmuch as it clearly sees the nature of the superior's command or desire and also sees that sin is excluded. Hence blind obedience always sees that the command is morally good." And again, "We should entirely conform our will and judgment to that of the superior, wherever no sin is discerned."

St. Thomas Aquinas in his SUMMA THEOLOGICA, Secunda Secundae, Question 104, Article 5, denotes three kinds of obedience: "Accordingly we may distinguish a threefold obedience; one, sufficient for salvation, and consisting in obeying when one is bound to obey; secondly, perfect obedience, which obeys in all things lawful; thirdly, indiscreet obedience, which obeys even in matters unlawful ... (Moreover), it is written (Acts 5:29): 'We ought to obey God rather than men.' Therefore superiors are not to be obeyed in all things."

In THE BOOK OF DESTINY – AN INTERPRETATION OF THE APOCALYPSE, by Father H. B. Kramer (Imprimatur January, 1956), Father Kramer states that "Satan will probably, through the evil world powers of the time, enforce the acceptance of unchristian morals, false doctrines, compromise with error. Through false doctrines and principles, Satan will mislead the clergy. Satan can vent more malice against the Church indirectly through bishops and priests than by his own power." And St. Pius X said: "A holy priest makes a holy people, and a priest who is not holy is not only useless, he is harmful to the world."

HAVE THERE NOT BEEN A FEW POPES WHO HAVE BEEN WICKED?

Yes, there have been. An elective monarchy, the Papacy attracted the ambition of worldly ecclesiastics and, for a time during the Middle Ages, became a prize for which rival monarchs intrigued, each trying to secure it for his own minion. Hence we find that there have been some few Popes incompetent and even wicked. Disastrous schisms have also occurred from time to time. (Schism is the action whereby one separates oneself from the Catholic Church by refusing to recognize the authority of the Pope.) The year 1054 is the date when the Eastern Christians (Near East) when into schism. This schism still exists – Greek Orthodox Church, Russian Orthodox Church, etc. In 1378 the Great Western Schism occurred in the Church, rival claimants to the Papacy sundering its unity. This schism endured until 1415. Any one of these schisms, any one of these Popes – if he had held a secular throne and were equally unfit for his office – would have brought the most powerful dynasty crashing to the ground. Moreover, the Papacy was threatened with another and, perhaps, greater, danger – the danger arising from ordinary human infirmity – for the Pope as a teacher, when not exercising his gift of infallibility, is liable to the errors of common men as we have already shown. We may, indeed, admit that, in the long history of the Papacy, there have been errors of policy, weaknesses, and wickedness which would have cost a *temporal* monarch his throne.

Because of these weak or bad Popes, the opponents of the Papacy conclude that the Papacy itself cannot be a Divine institution. But there were some very bad men among the high priests of the *Old Law* too, and yet no one contests their office of high priest as a *Divine* institution. The successors of St. Peter are frail human beings, just as *St. Peter himself was*, since the Primacy does not confer the prerogative of sinlessness or bravery. If among the 266 Popes who have ruled the Church up to our time, there were some whose lives were scandalous, God no doubt permitted this in order to show that *He Himself* rules the Church through the Popes; for not one of these so called "bad Popes" taught a single false doctrine or promulgated an ecclesiastical law that is morally reprehensible.

HAS THE CATHOLIC CHURCH HAD MANY SAINTLY PONTIFFS?

The first 56 Popes were proclaimed saints. The first 31 of these were martyred for the Faith, yet the Papacy went on. This was a miracle of miracles! The Catholic Faith was completely spread in the early ages of Christianity by the shedding of the blood of martyrs. From the year 33 to the year 306, there were eleven million Catholics martyred for the Faith. There have been 266 Popes in unbroken succession from St. Peter to Pope John Paul II. A total of 90 of these have been declared saints. For the last century and a half the throne of Peter has been occupied the majority of the time by great men, and by good men, by several geniuses, and by one canonized saint. The names and glories of Venerable Pius IX, Leo XIII, St. Pius X and Pius XI especially stand out. The humble Pope St. Pius X was elected to the Papal throne in 1903, died in 1914, and was canonized a saint in 1954. After his election he fearlessly entered every department of life in order to "renew all things in Christ." At his first consistory on November 9, 1903, he said: "We are convinced that many will resent our intention of taking an active part in world politics, but any impartial observer will realize that the Pope, to whom the supreme office of teacher has been entrusted by God, cannot remain indifferent to political affairs or separate them from the concerns of Faith and Morals. One of the primary duties of the Apostolic Office is to disprove and condemn erroneous doctrines and to oppose civil laws which are in conflict with the law of God, and so to preserve humanity from bringing about its own destruction."

Pope Pius XI (reigned 1922-1939) will be remembered for his official documents on the evils of Communism. He wrote 9 official documents on the subject. In 1937 his renowned Encyclical on "Atheistic Communism" was widely acclaimed in all free nations. It is an excellent summary of Marxism-Leninism. In it he stated that: "The all too imminent danger" of our own days is "Bolshevistic and Atheistic Communism, which aims at upsetting the social order and at undermining the very foundations of Christian civilization." He characterized it as a "satanic scourge," carrying on throughout the world "diabolical propaganda." To this day, Russia continues to spread her errors throughout the world.

THE HAND OF GOD IS SEEN IN THE MIRACLE OF THE CHURCH'S STABILITY

The durability of the Catholic Church is the marvel of her enemies. It is only the hand of God that could have brought her safely through such perils which have proved fatal to merely human institutions. Often death seemed to have come upon her, but, sustained by her Divine vitality, she cast off disease as a garment, and rose from her bed of sickness. She is like the house of which Christ speaks in the Gospel: "And the rain fell and the floods came, and they beat upon that house, and it fell not, for it was founded on a rock" (Matt. 7:25). Often have her children heard the demons' exultant cry that, at last, she was overwhelmed in the wave of death. But the tempest passed, and day broke anew, and the eyes of men beheld her still firmly fixed as of old on the rock of Peter, triumphant amid the wreckage of her enemies.

"There is not," says the *Protestant* writer Macaulay (Essay on Ranke's 'History of the Popes'), "and there never was on this earth, a work of human policy so well deserving of examination as the Roman Catholic Church. The proudest royal houses are but of yesterday, when compared with the line of the Supreme Pontiffs. That line we trace back in unbroken series from the Pope who crowned Napoleon in the nineteenth century to the Pope who crowned Pepin in the eighth; and far beyond the time of Pepin, the dynasty extends . . . The republic of Venice came next in antiquity. But the republic of Venice was modern when compared with the Papacy; and the republic of Venice is gone, and the Papacy remains . . . Nor do we see any sign which indicates that the term of her long domination is approaching. She saw the commencement of all the ecclesiastical establishments that now exist in the world; and we feel no assurance that she is not destined to see the end of them all . . . It is not strange that, in the year 1799, even sagacious observers should have thought that, at length, the hour of the Church of Rome was come. An infidel power ascendant, the Pope dying in captivity, the most illustrious prelates of France living in a foreign country on Protestant alms . . . But the end was not yet . . . Anarchy had had its day. A new order of things rose out of the confusion . . . and amidst them emerged the ancient religion. The arabs have a fable that the Great Pyramid was built by antediluvian kings, and alone, of all the works of men, bore the weight of the flood. Such as this was the fate of the Papacy. It had been buried under the great inundation; but its deep foundations had remained unshaken; and, when the waters abated, it appeared alone amidst the ruins of a world that had passed away. The Republic of Holland was gone, and the Empire of Germany, and . . . the House of Bourbon, and the parliaments and aristocracy of France. Europe was full of young creations, a French empire, a kingdom of Italy, a Confederation of the Rhine. Nor had the late events affected only territorial limits and political institutions. The distribution of property, the composition and spirit of society had, through a great part of Catholic Europe, undergone a complete change. But the unchangeable Church was still there."

We may summarize the argument as follows: (1) The Papacy, the foundation on which the Church is built, is the only institution which has survived all the vast social and political changes and revolutions in the life and government of Europe since the days of the Roman Emperors. (2) It has survived in spite of persecution, and political intrigue; in spite of heresy and schism among its subjects, in spite of the worldliness and the weakness or incompetency of some of the Popes. Such a survival is miraculous. The Papacy and the Church over which it presides must, therefore, be the work of God. "The Ark of the Church may be swept by the waves, but it can never sink because Christ is there" (St. Anselm).

ON OBEDIENCE DUE THE ROMAN CATHOLIC CHURCH

In the book "AN EXPOSITION AND DEFENSE OF ALL THE POINTS OF FAITH DISCUSSED AND DEFINED BY THE SACRED COUNCIL OF TRENT," by St. Alphonsus Maria Liguori, he states:

"A church which is not one in its doctrine and faith can never be the true church. Hence because truth must be one, of all the different churches only one can be the true one, and out of that church there is no salvation. Now, in order to determine which is this one true church, it is necessary to examine which is the church first founded by Jesus Christ. For, when the *first* is ascertained, it must be confessed that this alone is the True Church which, having been once the True Church, must always have been and must forever be. For to this first Church has been made the promise of the Savior that the gates of hell should never be able to overturn it (Matt. 16: 18).

"In the entire history of religion, we find that the Roman Catholic Church alone was the first church, and that the other false and heretical churches afterwards departed and separated from her . . . The innovators themselves do not deny that the Roman Church was the first which Jesus Christ founded. However, they say that the Roman Church was the true Church until the fifth century, or until it fell away because it had been corrupted by the Catholics. But how could that Church fail which St. Paul calls the pillar and ground of truth (1 Tim. 3:15)? No, the Church has not failed, and according to the promise of Christ it could not fail. But, pressed by this argument, the innovators have invented an answer: they say that the *visible* church has failed, but not the *invisible* church. But these doctrines are diametrically opposed to the Gospel. The innovators have been several times challenged to produce a single text of Sacred Scripture which would prove the existence of the invisible church which they invented, and we are unable to obtain any such text from them. How could they adduce such a text when, addressing His Apostles whom He left to the world as the propagators of His Church, Jesus Christ said: 'You are the light of the world. A city seated on a mountain cannot be hid' (Matt. 5:14). Thus He has declared that the Church cannot help but be visible to everyone . . . Were the Church at any time hidden and invisible, to whom would men have recourse in order to learn what they are to believe and to do? It was necessary that the Church and her Pastors be obvious and visible, principally in order that there might be an infallible judge to resolve all doubts and to whose decision everyone would necessarily submit. Otherwise there would be no sure rule of faith by which Christians could know the true dogmas of faith and the true precepts of morality, and among the faithful there would be endless disputes and controversies. 'And Christ gave some apostles, and others pastors and doctors, that henceforth we be no more children tossed to-and-fro and carried about with every wind of doctrine' (Eph. 4:11-14).

"What faith can we learn from false teachers when, in consequence of separating from the Church, they have no rule of faith? How often did Calvin change his opinions on the Eucharist! And, during his life, Luther was constantly contradicting himself: on the single article of the Eucharist, he fell into 33 contradictions. A single contradiction is sufficient to show that they did not have the Spirit of God: 'He cannot deny Himself' (II Tim. 2:13). In a word, take away the authority of the Church, and neither divine revelation nor natural reason itself is of any use, for each may be interpreted by every individual according to his own caprice. Do they not see that from this accursed liberty of conscience has arisen the immense variety of heretical and atheistic sects? I repeat: if you

50

take away obedience to the Church, there is no error which will not be embraced."

WHO THEN CAN BE SAVED?

"Strive to enter by the narrow gate: for many, I say to you, shall seek to enter, and shall not be able" (Luke 13:24).

Isaias, the great prophet, who foretold the coming of Our Lord, and the glorious establishing and perpetual flourishing of the Church of Christ, said the elect shall be as few as the forgotten ears of corn remaining on the stalks after the harvesting. Or as few as the bunches of grapes left on the vines after the pickers have finished their work. Or as few as the olives that remain after the shaking of the olive tree. Or as two or three berries on the top of a bough (Isaias 17:5-6). And "They that remain of the trees of his forest shall be so few that they shall easily be numbered, and a child shall write them down" (Isaias, 10:19). The Cure' d'Ars (St. John Marie Vianney), a poor parish priest in France, who was canonized by Pope Pius XI, in 1925, used these texts from Isaias in his sermons over and over, in order to help his people to realize how few are saved. He used them not only as applying in the Old Testament, but in the New Testament as well, for all time. As a result, the Cure' d'Ars won hundreds of souls to God.

Before going into other statements from Scripture on the fewness of the saved, it might be well here to say a few words about Holy Scripture and its interpretation. Holy Scripture, having God for its author ("inspired of God" 2 Tim 3:16), is free from all error. Pope Leo XIII in his encyclical "Providentissimus Deus" dated November 18, 1893 stated that "All of the books that the Church accepts as sacred and canonical, in their entirety, and together with all their parts, were written under the inspiration of the Holy Spirit . . . By its very nature inspiration not only excludes all error, but makes its presence as utterly impossible as it is for God, the supreme truth, to be the author of any error whatever. Vatican Council I made the unqualified statement that the books of the Old and the New Testament . . . have God for their author. This is the ancient and continuous belief of the Church; a belief, too, that was solemnly defined in the Councils of Florence and Trent and finally reaffirmed and more fully explained in Vatican Council I . . . With His supernatural power, God so stimulated and moved men to write, and so assisted them in their writing, that they properly understood and willed to write faithfully and express suitably with infallible truthfulness all that He ordered, but nothing more. Otherwise, God would not be the author of Sacred Scripture in its entirety . . . For this reason the Fathers and Doctors were convinced that the divine writings, precisely as written by the sacred writers, were free from all error."

And Our Lord Himself declared: "Scripture cannot be broken" (John 10:35).

Holy Scripture is to be interpreted literally. Pope Leo XIII calls attention in his encyclical "On the Study of Holy Scripture" to "the rule so wisely laid down by St. Augustine – not to depart from the literal and obvious sense except only where reason makes it untenable or necessity requires." And on June 30, 1909, the Biblical Commission under Pope St. Pius X gave this response concerning the historical character of the first chapters of Genesis. Emphasis is placed on the literal sense of the passage, which may not be called into question. Question: "In particular, may one question the literal historical sense when these . . . chapters . . . treat of facts that touch on fundamental points of the Christian religion?"
Response: "The literal, historical sense may not be questioned."

With the above as a preface, following are additional proofs on the fewness of the saved:

STATEMENTS FROM HOLY SCRIPTURE ON THE FEWNESS OF THE SAVED

"Many are called, but few are chosen" (Matt. 20:16).

"How narrow is the gate and strait the way that leadeth to life; and few there are who find it" (Matt. 7:14).

"Not everyone who saith to me 'Lord, Lord' shall enter the kingdom of Heaven, but he who doth the will of my Father who is in Heaven, he shall enter into the kingdom of Heaven" (Matt. 7:21).

"And if the just man shall *scarcely* be saved, where shall the ungodly and the sinner appear?" (1 Peter 4:18).

STATEMENTS OF SAINTS OF THE CHURCH ON THE FEWNESS OF THE SAVED

St. Jerome (420 A.D.), Saint and Doctor of the Church: "Of a hundred thousand sinners who continue in sin till death, scarcely one will be saved" (Sermon 255, E.B. app.).

St. John Chrysostom (407), the "golden-mouthed" Doctor of the Church, writing about the salvation of bishops and priests, said: "I do not speak rashly, but as I feel and think. I do not think that many priests are saved, but that those who perish are far more numerous. The reason is that the office requires a great soul. For there are many things to make a priest swerve from rectitude, and he requires great vigilance on every side. Do you not perceive how many qualities a bishop must have that he may be apt to teach; patient towards the wicked, firm and faithful in teaching the word? How many difficulties herein. Moreover the loss of others is imputed to him. I need say no more . . . "

St. Thomas Aquinas (1274): "A select few are to be saved" (Summa Theo. 1a, qu. 23, Art. 7, ad 3).

St. Francis Xavier (1552), the great apostle to India and Japan, said in his Prayer for the Conversion of the Infidels: "Behold, O Lord, how to Thy dishonor Hell is being filled with these souls . . . " (See Father Francis Lasance's prayer book "With God" published by Benziger Brothers, Imprimatur 1954).

St. Louis-Marie de Montfort (1716): "The number of the elect is so small – so small – that were we to know how small it is, we should faint away with grief. The number of the elect is so small that were God to assemble them together, He would cry to them, as He did of old by the mouth of His prophet, 'Gather yourselves together, one by one' – one from this province, one from that kingdom."

STATEMENTS FROM SCRIPTURE ON NON-CHRISTIANS
(Mohammedans, Hindus, Buddhists, Jews, etc.)

"He that believeth in the Son hath life everlasting: but he that believeth not the Son shall not see life: but the wrath of God abideth on him" (John 3:36).

"I am the way and the truth and the life. No man cometh to the Father but by me" (John 14:6).

"He that believeth in the Son of God hath the testimony of God in himself. He that believeth not the Son maketh him a liar: because he believeth not in the testimony which God hath testified of His Son. And this is the testimony that God hath given to us eternal life. And this life is in His Son. He that hath the Son hath life, He that hath not the Son hath not life" (1 John 5:10-12).

"Neither is there salvation in any other (than in the name of our Lord Jesus Christ). For there is no other name under heaven given to men, whereby we must be saved" (Acts 4:12).

"Jesus answered: 'Amen, amen, I say to thee, unless a man be born again of water and the Holy Ghost, he cannot enter into the kingdom of God" (John 3:5).

STATEMENTS FROM SCRIPTURE ON NON-CATHOLICS

Christ commissioned His Apostles to "go into the whole world and preach the Gospel to every creature" (Mark 16:15), "teaching them to observe all things whatsoever I have commanded you" (Matt. 28:20). "He that believeth and is baptized shall be saved; but he that believeth not shall be condemned" (Mark 16:16). It is manifest from this that it is not enough to believe in just the *person* of Jesus Christ; we must also believe His doctrines and obey His words – those divine truths He entrusted to His Church, among which are the seven sacraments. All creatures are therefore obliged to become members of Christ's Church for "He that believeth not shall be condemned" (Mark 16:16). And "If he will not hear the Church, let him be to thee as the heathen and the publican" (Matt. 18:17). That is, he is not to be considered a Christian at all, and is therefore, *according to Christ's own judgment*, outside the pale of salvation. Remember, Christ established only *one* Church, and this one true Church is of apostolic origin; and He said: "He that heareth you, heareth me: and he that despiseth you, despiseth me" (Luke 10:16).

Christ, speaking of those who were not yet joined in the communion of His Church, but whom He foreknew would make a good use of the graces He would give them for that purpose, says, "Other sheep I have who are not of this fold, them also I *must* bring, and they shall hear my voice, and there shall be one fold and one shepherd" (John 10:16). Here he plainly declares that all those of His sheep, who are not yet of His fold, *must* be brought to it, as a necessary condition of their salvation. In consequence of this settled disposition of the divine providence, no sooner did the apostles begin to preach the gospel, than immediately "The Lord added daily to the Church *those being saved*" (Acts 2:47, Greek translation). This evidently shows that all who are not added to the Church, are out of all hope of salvation. The same was true of all souls from the time of the foundation of the Israelite religion to the time of the establishment of Christ's Church, who were not adherents of the Jewish Faith, for "Salvation is of the Jews," Christ said to the Samaritan woman (John 4:22). (You mean to say that in the Old Dispensation you had to believe in the **Jewish Faith** in order to be saved? Yes! That's what Jesus **said,** didn't He? And "He cannot deny Himself" 2 Tim. 2:13.)

THE TEACHING OF THE CHURCH ON THE DOGMA OF SALVATION

Has the Roman Catholic Church, herself, ever spoken on this point in a solemn and infallible manner? Yes, she has made three infallible pronouncements (ex cathedra definitions) on the subject. These definitions must be believed under pain of excommunication. They have been taken directly from the "Enchiridion Symbolorum." The "Enchiridion Symbolorum," or "The Handbook of the Creed," contains all the major pronouncements of the Popes – either defining alone or at the head of their bishops in Council – and all the ex cathedra definitions. The theologians refer to the Enchiridion usually as "Denzinger," as it was compiled by Father Henry Denzinger. Remember, as previously stated, the Pope is infallible only when he acts as head of the Church, making it clear that he is speaking ex cathedra (from the Chair of Peter) (2) in defining a doctrine on faith or morals (3) with the intent of binding the whole Church. (On July 18, 1870,

Vatican Council I in its "First Dogmatic Constitution on the Church of Christ" solemnly defined the infallible authority of the Roman Pontiff: " . . . We, with the approval of the sacred council, teach and define that it is a divinely revealed dogma: that the Roman Pontiff, when he speaks ex cathedra, that is, when, acting in the office of shepherd and teacher of all Christians, he defines, by virtue of his supreme apostolic authority, doctrine concerning faith or morals to be held by the universal Church, possesses through the divine assistance promised to him in the person of St. Peter, the infallibility with which the divine Redeemer willed his Church to be endowed in defining doctrine concerning faith or morals; and that such definitions of the Roman Pontiff are therefore irreformable because of their nature, but not because of the agreement of the Church.")

The following, then, are the three ex cathedra definitions which fix *for all time* the teaching of the Solemn Magisterium on the necessity of the Church for salvation. Notice that each pronouncement is more definite and emphatic than the one before it:

At the Fourth Lateran Council, in 1215 (the Twelfth Ecumenical Council), Pope Innocent III defined against the Albigenses and other heretics, declaring: "There is but one universal Church of the faithful, outside of which *no one at all* can be saved" (Denzinger No. 430).

Pope Boniface VIII, 1294-1303, in his Bull "Unam Sanctam," November 18, 1302, expounds the doctrine of the Church, and ends with an infallible definition: "Urged by faith, we are obliged to believe and to hold that the Church is one, holy, catholic, and also apostolic. We firmly believe in her, and we confess absolutely that outside of her there is neither salvation nor the remission of sins, as the Spouse in the Canticles (6:8) proclaims: 'One is my dove, my perfect one. She is the only one of her mother, the chosen of her that bore her,' who represents one mystical body, whose head is Christ, and the head of Christ is God. In her there is one Lord, one faith, one baptism. There was indeed at the time of the deluge only one Ark of Noah, prefiguring that One Church, which Ark, having been finished to a single cubit, had only one pilot and guide, i.e., Noah, outside of which as we read, all that subsisted on the earth was destroyed . . . Furthermore, *We declare, say, define and pronounce* that it is absolutely necessary for the salvation of *every* human creature to be subject to the Roman Pontiff" (Denzinger Nos. 468, 469).

Pope Eugene IV, in the Council of Florence, decreed in the Bull, Cantate Domino, February 4, 1441: "The most Holy Roman Church firmly *believes, professes and preaches,* that none of those existing outside the Catholic Church, not only pagans, but also Jews and heretics and schismatics, can have a share in life eternal; but that they will go into the eternal fire, which was prepared for the devil and his angels, unless before death they are joined with Her; and that so important is the unity of this ecclesiastical body that only those remaining within this unity can profit by the sacraments of the Church unto salvation, and they alone can receive an eternal recompense for their fasts, their almsgiving, their other works of Christian piety, and the duties of a Christian soldier. No one, let his almsgiving be as great as it may, no one, even if he pour out his blood for the name of Christ, can be saved, unless he remain within the bosom and the unity of the Catholic Church" (Denz. 714).

With regard to doctrines of the Church, the First Vatican Council in its "Dogmatic Constitution on the Catholic Faith" dated April 24, 1870, Chapter 4, states: "For the doctrine of faith *as revealed by God* has not been presented to men as a philosophical system to be perfected by human ingenuity; it was presented as *a divine trust* given to the bride of Christ to be faithfully kept and infallibly interpreted. It also follows that any meaning of the sacred dogmas that has once been declared by holy Mother Church, must always be retained; and there must never be any deviation from that meaning on the specious grounds of a more profound understanding." And Canon 3 on this chapter states: "If anyone says that as science progresses it is sometimes possible for dogmas that have been proposed by the Church to receive a different meaning from the one which the Church understood and understands: let him be anathema" (Denz. No. 1818). As an illustration, let us take Pope Innocent's pronouncement: "There is but one universal Church of the faithful, outside of which no one at all can be saved." "No one at all" means "none." If even *one* person outside the Church is granted salvation, then the sense and meaning of this dogma is changed. It would then read: ". . . outside of which *some* can be saved".

The three dogmatic pronouncements above were not new doctrines added to the Deposit of Faith. All the truths of the Catholic Faith were given to us by the time of the death of the last apostle, St. John, in the year 99 A.D. This is known as the "Deposit of Faith." So the doctrine on salvation was part of that "Deposit of Faith" from the time of Christ, and at the beginning of the Church. ("He who does not believe shall be condemned," Mk. 16:16.) The doctrines of the Church can never change. They are today precisely what they were at the beginning of the Church. "Faith, once transmitted," says St. Jude Thaddeus, "is delivered forever" (Jude 1:3). It is impossible to revise, reform, or change any doctrine in Christianity. Men may accept the doctrine Christ taught, or reject it. *But if they alter it, it ceases to be the gospel of Christ.* Humanity must conform to God's teachings; not adjust those teachings to suit itself. The Church grieves that so many who should be Catholic are not. But to win them, she cannot change the doctrines Christ committed to her keeping. It is useless to convert people to a faith that has changed – and to which the promises of Christ were never made.

So, when a truth of the Church has been called into question, it has been necessary for the Pope to define it; that is, to re-express the doctrine in more exact, precise, language so that there can be no further doubt about its meaning. In other words, the purpose of a definition is to *clarify*.

No future Pope or Council can ever change the sense or meaning of a dogma of the Church. If such ever *appears* to have been done, it can be shown that the Pope is not speaking infallibly. Only when he is speaking infallibly is he guarded by the Holy Ghost against error.

THE TEACHING OF THE SAINTS ON THE DOGMA OF SALVATION

The saints of Christianity, in every age, have spoken on the subject of salvation in the same strain; that is, they hold exactly the same meaning, which is: No one can be saved outside actual, formal membership in the one true visible Roman Catholic Church.

St. Ignatius (107 A.D.), disciple of the Apostles, was the third Bishop of Antioch. He governed the Church there for 40 years. In his Epistle to the Philadelphians, he says, "Those who make a separation (from the Church) shall not inherit the kingdom of God."

St. Cyprian (258), Bishop of Carthage, wrote: ". . . Whosoever separates himself from the Church is joined to an adulterer and has cut himself off from the promises made to the Church; no one who quits the Church of Christ will attain to the rewards of Christ. He is a stranger, profane, an enemy. He cannot have God for his Father who has not the Church for his mother. If anyone who was outside the Ark of Noah was able to escape (and we know no one was), then whosoever is outside the Church escapes." And in his book on the "Unity of the Church," he wrote: "If such (heretics or schismatics) should even suffer martyrdom for the name of Christ, they would not expiate their crime. There can be no such thing as a martyr out of the Church. Though they should be thrown into the fire, or be exposed to the fury of wild beasts, such a death will never be esteemed a crown of their faith and constancy, but rather a punishment of their perfidy. Such a man may be put to death, but cannot be crowned . . . If the schismatic should suffer out of the church of Christ, he will never thence become entitled to the recompense which none can claim who are not in it. There is but one God, one Christ, one Church, one Faith, and one entire body of Christian people. Whatever shall be separated from the fountain of life, can have no life remaining in it, after having lost all communication with its vital principle."

St. Augustine (430), the great Bishop, Father and Doctor of the Church, said in a sermon to the people of Caesarea: "No man can find salvation except in the Catholic Church. Outside the Catholic Church he can find everything except salvation. He can have dignities, he can have the Sacraments, can sing 'Alleluia,' answer 'Amen,' accept the Gospels, have faith in the Name of the Father, the Son and the Holy Ghost, and preach it, too, but never except in the Catholic Church can he find salvation." And in his Epistle Ad Feliciam, he says: "In the Catholic Church there are both good and bad. But those that are separated from her, as long as their opinions are opposite hers, cannot be good. For though the conversation of some of them appears commendable, yet their very separation from the Church makes them bad, according to that of our Saviour 'He that is not with me is against me; and he that gathers not with me scattereth' " (Luke 11:23).

St. Thomas Aquinas (1274), Doctor of the Church. In his treatise "Against the Errors of the Greeks," St. Thomas wrote: "To be subject to the Roman Pontiff is necessary for salvation."

St. Peter Canisius (1597), Doctor of the Church. He was the great leader of the Counter-Reformation against Protestants in German countries in the Sixteenth Century. In his Catechism of Catholic Doctrine, he says, "Outside of this communion, as outside the Ark of Noah, there is absolutely no salvation for mortals: not to Jews or Pagans, who never received the faith of the Church; not to heretics who, having received it, forsook or corrupted it; not to schismatics who left the peace and unity of the Church; ... For the rule of Cyprian and Augustine is certain: he will not have God for his Father who would not have the Church for his Mother."

THE TEACHING OF THE POPES OF THE TWENTIETH CENTURY ON THE DOGMA OF SALVATION

Pope Leo XIII's last official words: "This is Our last lesson to you: receive it, engrave it in your minds, all of you: *by God's commandment* salvation is to be found nowhere but in the Church." (Allocution for the 25th Anniversary of His Election, February 20, 1903).

St. Pius X: "It is Our duty to recall to everyone, great and small, the absolute necessity we are under to have recourse to the Church to effect our eternal salvation" (From his Encyclical 'Jucunda sane', March 12, 1904).

Pope Pius XI: "If any man does not enter the Catholic Church, or if any man departs from her, he is far from the hope of life and salvation" (Encyclical 'Fostering True Religious Unity,' January 6, 1928). "When it is a question of life and salvation, we can and we must say of the Church what St. Peter said of Jesus Christ: 'Neither is there salvation in any other' " (Autograph Letter 'Dobbiamo intrattenerla,' April 26, 1931).

Pope Pius XII: The Church alone is the entrance to salvation; she alone, by herself, and under the protection and guidance of the Holy Spirit, is the source of truth." (Allocution to the students of the Gregorianum, October 17, 1953).

62

Pope John XXIII: "The Savior himself is the door of the sheepfold: 'I am the door of the sheep.' Into this fold of Jesus Christ, no man may enter unless he be led by the Sovereign Pontiff; and only if they be united to him can men be saved, for the Roman Pontiff is the Vicar of Christ and his personal representative on earth." (Homily to the Bishops and Faithful Assisting at the Ceremonies of His Papal Coronation, November 4, 1958).

Pope Paul VI: "This would be the right place for a study of the Mystical Body of Christ, which is the Church. Do not all the baptized belong to the Church? And is not the Church one only? Yes, the Council answers, but membership in the Church requires other conditions besides baptism, such as identical faith and unity of communion. The Catholic Church alone is the Body of Christ, of which He is Head and Savior. Outside this Body, the Holy Spirit does not give life to anyone. Those who are hostile to unity do not participate in divine charity. Those outside the Church do not possess the Holy Spirit. And those who wish to possess the Holy Spirit take good care not to remain outside the Church. A Christian must fear nothing so much as to be separated from the Body of Christ. If, in fact, he is separated from the Body of Christ, he is not one of His members: and, not being one of His members, he is not fed by His Spirit." (General Audiences of May 15, 1974 and June 12, 1974, as quoted in The Wanderer of May 30, and July 4, 1974).

Pope John Paul I: "It is difficult to accept some truths, because the truths of faith are of two kinds: some pleasant, others unpalatable to our spirit. For example, it is pleasant to hear that God has so much tenderness for us, even more tenderness than a mother for her children. Other truths, on the contrary, are hard to accept. God must punish if I resist. That is not agreeable, but it is a truth of faith. There is one last difficulty: the Church. It is clear that Jesus and the Church are the *same thing:* indissoluble, inseparable. Christ and the Church are *only* one thing. It is not possible to say: 'I believe in Jesus, I accept Jesus, but I do not accept the Church.' When the poor Pope, when the bishops, the priests, propose The Doctrine; they are merely helping Christ. It is not *our* doctrine; it is Christ's; we must merely guard it and present it." (General Audience of September 13, 1978, as quoted by Daughters of St. Paul in their St. Paul Edition of "The Message of John Paul I", 1978, pp. 106-107).

Pope John Paul II: "We have to be conscious of, and absorb, this fundamental and revealed truth, contained in the phrase hallowed by Tradition: There is no salvation outside the Church. From her alone flows surely and fully the life-giving force destined, in Christ and in His Spirit, to renew the whole of humanity, and therefore directing every human being to become a part of the Mystical Body of Christ." (Radio Message on the Eighth Centenary of St. Francis of Assisi, October 3, 1981).

(I am not quoting Pope John Paul II's weak points, where he is speaking as an individual theologian – i.e., *not defining*. I am only quoting his words which *support* this defined dogma of the Faith – the *official* position of the Magisterium).

HOW DISBELIEF IN THE DOGMA OF SALVATION CAME ABOUT

It is only of late that disbelief in the necessity of belonging to the Catholic Church for salvation has appeared among those who call themselves Catholic. This is one of the greatest grounds for its condemnation. This loose way of thinking is a new doctrine; it was unheard of from the beginning; it is directly opposite the uniform doctrine of all the great lights of the Church in all former ages. These great and holy men knew no other language on the subject but what was spoken before them by Christ and His apostles; they knew their Divine Master had declared, "He that believeth not shall be condemned"; they heard His apostle thundering out a dreadful anathema on any one, even though an angel from heaven, who should dare to, alter the gospel He had preached (Galatians 1:8). And they constantly held to the same language, the same sense, the same meaning.

The enemy came "inside" the Church about one hundred and fifty years ago when several loosely worded sentences of Pope Pius IX in two encyclicals and in one allocution (in which he was not defining) were used by liberals as the basis of their teaching that there is salvation outside the Catholic Church. The liberals' theories have now taken the place of dogma in people's minds. So now, in our day, bishops, priests, theologians, and canon lawyers insist that distinctions be made with regard to the doctrine "Outside the Church there is no salvation." These distinctions are so involved, contorted, fantastic, and dishonest that the dogma has finally emerged completely changed. To the straightforward question: Is there or is there not salvation outside the Catholic Church? the answer, after this manipulation of doctrine, would have to be: Yes, there is salvation outside the Catholic Church. We have now arrived at the exact opposite of the infallible pronouncements of the Popes. Men welcomed the change of teaching, as it gave license for a softer life.

Another crucial point at which heresy entered the fold of the Catholic Church in the United States and backwashed to the dying faith of Europe and the rest of the world, was through the teaching of the doctrine known as "Baptism of Desire" in the Baltimore Catechism. The Baltimore Catechism was concocted at the Third Plenary Council of Baltimore, Maryland in 1884 by a group of American Bishops under the influence of James Cardinal Gibbons, Archbishop of Baltimore. Cardinal Gibbons' main ambition was to show that Catholicism was good Americanism. It is for that reason that he went out of his way to take such metaphorical expressions in theology as "Baptism of Desire" and "Baptism of Blood" and put them side by side with Baptism of Water as sufficient for salvation, in precise

denial of Our Lord's own words to the contrary that
"Unless a person be born again of water and the Holy
Spirit, he cannot enter the Kingdom of Heaven" (John 3:5).
As a consequence, every little Catholic child in a Catholic
school, from the time of Cardinal Gibbons on, has been
required to say, in answer to the question, "How many
kinds of Baptism are there?": "There are three kinds of
Baptism: Baptism of Water, Baptism of Desire, and
Baptism of Blood." That is heresy. There is only "one Lord,
one Faith, *one* Baptism" (Eph. 4:5). The Council of Vienne
explicitly defines that this one Baptism, which is
administered by water, is the one which must be faithfully
confessed by all. "All the faithful must confess only one
Baptism, which regenerates in Christ all the baptized, just
as there is one God and one faith. We believe that this
Sacrament, celebrated in *water,* and in the name of the
Father, Son, and Holy Ghost is necessary for children and
for grown-up people alike, as the perfect remedy for
salvation" (Council of Vienne). Neither "Baptism of Desire"
nor "Baptism of Blood" are salvational substitutes for
water Baptism. *Neither is a sacrament of the Church.
Neither was instituted by Jesus Christ. No one can receive
any of the other sacraments by reason of having received
these so-called "Baptisms."* Baptism of *water* is the initial
requirement for the reception of all the other sacraments,
and the only door to entrance into the Church.

Baptism of Desire means *a desire for* Baptism of Water, and
a full intent to receive it, for "Unless a man be born again
of water and the Holy Ghost he cannot enter into the
kingdom of God"(John 3:5). To "be born again of
water"means to be born again by *a spiritual regeneration* in
God, and this is absolutely necessary to salvation. The
erroneous and deceptious evasions called "desires" are
without foundation from traditional Catholic theology and
are not to be found in Scripture. All desires for the
sacraments must end in the *actual reception* of them, or
else the desire was but a "good intention." The road to hell
is paved with "good intentions"!

St. Gregory Nazianzen stated: "Of those who fail to be baptized, some are utterly animal or bestial, according to whether they are foolish or wicked. . . Others know and honor the gift of Baptism; but they delay, some out of carelessness, some because of insatiable passion. Still others are not able to receive Baptism, perhaps because of infancy, or some perfectly involuntary circumstance which prevents their receiving the gift, even if they desire it. . . I think the first group will have to suffer punishment, not only for their other sins, but also for their contempt of Baptism. The second group will also be punished, but less, because it was not through wickedness so much as through foolishness that they brought about their own failure. The third group will neither be glorified nor punished by the Just Judge; for, although they are un-Sealed, they are not wicked. They are not so much wrong-doers as ones who have suffered a loss . . . If you were able to judge a man who intends to commit murder solely by his *intention* and without any *act* of murder, then you could likewise reckon as baptized one who *desired* Baptism without having received Baptism. But, since you cannot do the former, how can you do the latter? . . . If you prefer, we will put it this way: if, in your opinion, *desire* has equal power with *actual* Baptism, then make the same judgment in regard to Glory. You would then be satisfied to desire Glory, as though that longing itself were Glory. Do you suffer any damage by not attaining the *actual Glory,* as long as you have a *desire* for it? I cannot see it!" ("Oration on the Holy Lights" XL:23, "Patrologiae Cursus Completus": Series Graeca, Fr. J. P. Magne,Paris: 1866; and "The Faith of the Early Fathers," Fr. William Jurgens, Collegeville, MN: Liturgical Press, 1979, II, 1012).

The Council of Trent, in its Second Canon on Baptism, declares with the majestic authority of the Church: "If anyone shall say that true and natural water is not of necessity in Baptism, and therefore shall turn those words of our Lord Jesus Christ, 'Unless one be born again of water and the Holy Ghost' (John 3:5) into some metaphor, let him be anathema." Douay-Rheims Catholic Bible, footnote on John 3:5, states: "The ancient Fathers, and particularly St. Augustine in divers places, from these words, prove the necessity of giving baptism to infants: and by Christ's adding water, is excluded a metaphorical baptism." Therefore, metaphorical water is forbidden under pain of heresy. And what is "Baptism of Desire," as the liberals teach it, but metaphorical water dishonestly substituting itself for the innocent requirement of Jesus Christ?

The Council of Trent, in its Fifth Canon on Baptism, declares: "If anyone says baptism is optional, that is, not necessary for salvation: let him be anathema." And the Catechism of the Council of Trent states that: "The *universal and absolute necessity* of Baptism our Saviour has declared in these words: 'Unless a man be born again of water and the Holy Ghost, he cannot enter into the kingdom of God.' " And it further states that: ". . . the law of Baptism, as established by our Lord, extends to *all*, so that unless they are regenerated to God through the grace of Baptism . . . they are born to eternal misery and destruction."

The above arguments prove, too, the heresy of the so called "Baptism of Blood" as a substitute for sacramental Baptism in attaining Heaven, but here are additional proofs: Pope Eugene IV's Bull, Cantate Domino: ". . . no one, *even if he pour out his blood for the name of Christ,* can be saved, unless he remain within the bosom and the unity of the Catholic Church." And St. Cyprian (d. 258 A.D.) states: "Nay, though they should suffer death for the confession of the Name, the guilt of such men is not removed *even by their blood;* the grievous irremissible sin of schism is not purged even by martyrdom. No martyr can he be who is not in the Church. . . Such a man may be put to death; crowned he cannot be . . ." (From the book "Ancient Christian Writers").

Heretics use the following verse to show that martyrs can be saved without the Sacrament of Baptism: "He that findeth his life shall lose it; and he that loses his life for My sake, shall find it" (Matt. 10:39). St. Ambrose and St. Chrysostom show it to mean *mortification:* "Behold the great losses that befall such as love their souls above measure; and on the contrary, the advantages that follow from hating them as they ought" (St. John Chrysostom). "But if he continues moderately happy as to temporal concerns till death, and places his affections on them, he hath found life here, but shall lose it in the next world. But he that shall, for the love of Christ, deprive himself of the pleasures of this life, shall receive the reward of a hundred-fold in the next" (St. Ambrose).

Likewise, "Belonging to the *Soul* of the Church" (though outside the fold) is a heresy. This heresy, which has been spread by theologians since the nineteenth century, resulted from a misconstruction of Cardinal Bellarmine's thesis that the Mystical Body of Christ – His Church – like the human body, comprises both a visible body and an invisible soul, but in no sense intended that those outside the communion with Christ's Church are of the soul of this Mystical Body. The expression "the soul of the Church" is but a metaphor. It was never intended to be used in more than a metaphorical sense, and that was the sense in which St. Augustine first used it. It was never intended to be a partitioning of the Church into two parts, soul and body, of which the fuller members belong to both parts, and the lesser members to just one of the parts. But that is the way it is being used by the liberal teachers of theology in the seminaries of the United States today, so as to save them the embarrassment of having to teach Protestants unequivocally where it is they must be saved. It is well known that Pope Pius XII, in his encyclical of June 29, 1943 on the Mystical Body insists that the only true sense in which we can use the phrase "soul of the Church," is to apply it to the *Holy Spirit:* "This presence and activity of the Spirit of Jesus Christ is tersely and vigorously described by Our predecessor of immortal memory, Leo XIII, in his Encyclical Letter 'Divinum Illud' in these words: 'Let it suffice to say, that as Christ is the head of the

Church, so is the Holy Spirit her soul' " (Pope Pius XII's Encyclical "The Mystical Body of Christ," Page 19, #61). And Pope Leo XIII's Encyclical "On the Unity of the Church" dated June 20, 1896, states: "Does the soul follow the amputated member? As long as it was in the body it lived; separated it loses its life. So the Christian is a Catholic as long as he lives in the body; cut off from it he becomes a heretic. The life of the spirit does not follow the amputated member."

The perversion of modernism and liberalism within the Church are everywhere present, but are especially strong, and appear to have gained their greatest strength within the ranks of the *American* clergy. One era in American Catholic history which the dominant liberalist sect of today would like to forget was that time at the turn of the century, when the Universal Church was so disrupted and agitated by their heretical and corrupting influences, that His Holiness Pope Leo XIII was obliged to issue a sharp rebuke in the form of the Apostolic Letter "Testem Benevolentiae" condemning the erroneous opinions which were being propagated under the name "Americanism." In the letter, Pope Leo XIII states: "The principles on which the new opinions . . . are based may be reduced to this, that, in order the more easily to bring over to Catholic doctrine those who dissent from it, the Church ought to adapt Herself somewhat to our advanced civilization, and, relaxing her ancient rigor, show some indulgence to modern popular theories and methods. Many think that this is to be understood not only with regard to the rule of life, but also the doctrines in which the Deposit of Faith is contained. For they contend that it is opportune, in order to work in a more attractive way upon the wills of those who are not in accord with us, to pass over certain heads of doctrine, as if of lesser moment, or to so soften them that they may not have the same meaning which the Church has invariably held. Now, Beloved Sons, few words are needed to show how reprehensible is the plan that is thus conceived, if we do consider the character and *origin* of the doctrine which the Church hands down to us. . . The First

Vatican Council says: 'By the Divine and Catholic Faith those things are to be believed, which are contained in the Word of God either written or handed down, and are proposed by the Church whether in solemn decision or by the ordinary universal Magisterium, to be believed as having been Divinely revealed.' Far be it then for anyone to diminish or for any reason whatever to pass over anything of this *Divinely delivered doctrine;* whosoever would do so, would rather wish to alienate Catholics from the Church, than to bring over to the Church those who dissent from it. Let them return; indeed, nothing is dearer to our heart; let all those who are wandering far from the sheepfold of Christ return; but let it not be by any other road than that which Christ has pointed out."

Now that the world is overrun with heresy, and all distinctions between the faithful and the infidel obliterated, it is convenient to men's ease and acceptable to their cowardice to regard the faith as one of *many* saving opinions, and the Church as one of many saving institutions. Men will make light of the enormous privileges and of the exclusive rights of the Church, either out of human respect or as an easy way of diminishing the difficulties of a problem which they are unable to solve and do not like to face. We must look at the Church habitually as the sole ark in the deluge of the world, the solitary mistress of salvation. *We do not bind God further than He has been pleased to bind Himself.* We do not limit the far reaching excesses of His mercy, but we must remember that there is no salvation whatever outside the Roman Church. We must be jealous of the uncompromising simplicity of this old-fashioned doctrine. We must be suspicious of all the fine words, and specious theories which the spirit of the times suggest. We must be misled by no circumstances of time or place, by no prevalence of heresy, by no arguments drawn from consequences. The sins of men cannot change the truth of God.

Back in the third century, St. Cyprian, writing on "The Unity of the Catholic Church" states: "The enemy snatches away people from within the Church herself, and while they think that coming close to the light they have now done with the night of the world, he plunges them unexpectedly into darkness of another kind. They still call themselves Christians after abandoning the Gospel of Christ and the observance of His Law; though walking in darkness they think they still enjoy the light. The enemy cajoles and deceives them; as the Apostle says, he transforms himself into an angel of light, and primes his servants to act as the servants of justice, to call the night day, and damnation salvation, to teach recklessness under the pretext of hope, disbelief under colour of the faith, antichrist under the name of Christ, so that by lies they have all the appearance of truth, they undermine the truth with trickery. All this has come about, dearest brethren, because men do not go back to the *origin* of the Christian realities, because they do not look for their source, nor keep to the teaching of their heavenly Master."

THE FOLLOWING OBJECTIONS ARE ANSWERED

(1) When you say "Outside the Church there is no salvation," it depends on what you mean by "Church."

A Catholic child will have no trouble in answering from the Catechism: "The Church is the congregation of all the faithful, who, being baptized, profess the same doctrine, partake of the same sacraments, and are governed by their lawful pastors, under one visible head, the Pope" (From "The Large Catechism of the Catholic Religion" by Joseph Deharbe, S.J.). In the Encyclical Letter "The Mystical Body of Christ," Pope Pius XII states: "If we would define and describe this true Church of Jesus Christ – which is the One, Holy, Catholic, Apostolic, Roman Church – we shall find no expression more noble, more sublime or more divine than the phrase which calls it 'the Mystical Body of Jesus Christ.' This title is derived from and is, as it were, the fair flower of the repeated teaching of Sacred Scripture

72

(Eph. 5:23,24) and the Holy Fathers. 'The Church is visible because she is a Body' Pope Leo XIII's Encyclical 'Satis Cognitus' asserts. Hence they err in a matter of divine truth who imagine the Church to be invisible, intangible . . . by which many Christian communities, though they differ from each other in their profession of faith, are united by a bond that eludes the senses. Only those are really to be included as members of the Church who have been baptized, and profess the true faith, and who have not unhappily withdrawn from body-unity or for grave faults been excluded by legitimate authority . . . It follows that those who are divided in Faith (beliefs), or government, cannot be living in one body such as this, and cannot be living the life of its one divine spirit."

"But in every nation he who feareth Him and worketh justice is acceptable to Him" (Acts of the Apostles, 10:35). The footnote to this verse in Catholic Douay Bible, states: "That is to say, not only Jews, but Gentiles also, of what nation soever, are acceptable to God, if they fear him and work justice. But then *true* faith is always to be presupposed, without which (saith St. Paul, Heb. 11:6) it is impossible to please God. ("Teach them to observe all things whatsoever I have commanded you," Mt. 28:20) Beware then of the error of those who would infer from this passage that men of all religions may be pleasing to God. For since none but the true religion can be from God, all other religions must be from the father of lies, and therefore highly displeasing to the God of truth."

(2)   "Judge not, that you may not be judged" (Matt. 7:1).

This scripture does not forbid a judgment on the weaknesses of sinners. The spiritual works of mercy include: to admonish the sinner, instruct the ignorant, counsel the doubtful. Matthew 7:1 forbids *rash* judgment, for Jesus says: "With what judgment you judge, you shall be judged" (Matt. 7:2). If we give just judgment, we shall be judged justly by God. If we judge rashly, then He will judge us likewise. Following Jesus's counsel in St. John 5:30, we will not make a rash judgment. He says: "As I hear, so I judge. And my judgment is just: because I seek not my own will, but the will of him that sent me." Here Jesus is saying that an intelligent and just judgment will be to *hear,* and then to judge whether the soul is sick or healthy. When heresy is spoken, then we know charity demands that we then assist our neighbor "to come to the knowledge of the truth" because this is the "will of God" (1 Timothy 2:4).

(3) God is love, God is merciful!

The scriptures say that and more. They tell us that God is also infinitely *just* against those who oppose His grace, light, inspirations, Church, and Gospel. "But to God the wicked and his wickedness are hateful alike" (Wis. 14:9); "And my eye shall not spare, neither will I show mercy: But I will lay thy ways upon thee, and thy abominations shall be in the midst of thee" (Ezechiel 7:9); "You have despised all my counsel, and have neglected my reprehensions. I also will laugh in your destruction, and will mock when that comes to you which you feared" (Prov. 1:25-26); "Not everyone that saith to me, Lord, Lord, shall enter into the kingdom of heaven: but he that doth the will of my Father. . ." (Matt. 7:21); "And if he refuse to hear them, appeal to the Church, but if he refuse to hear even the Church, let him be to thee as the heathen and the publican" (Matt. 18:17).

(4) When we say that there is no salvation outside the Church, we mean that the Church is the "ordinary" means of salvation: One cannot "limit" God you know.

No doubt God could have saved all mankind through the merits of any one thing Jesus did or suffered, without requiring such a severe sacrifice from Him as His death upon the Cross. But the great question for us is to know what God *has done.* Now, we have seen from the whole tenor of revelation that God has appointed true faith in Jesus Christ, and the being a member of His Church, as conditions of salvation; that He has appointed them as essential conditions, so that none will or can be saved without them; that the word of God points out no other possible way by which man can be saved: nay, that whatever extraordinary ways He may sometimes take to bring people to His Church, it is impossible He should, in fact, have reserved any extraordinary means of salvation for those who live and die not joined in communion with the Church by true Faith, otherwise He would contradict Himself, and give the lie to His own words, which is absolutely impossible. "He cannot deny Himself" (2 Timothy 2:13). "God is not a man, that he should lie, nor as the son of man, that he should be changed. Hath he said then, and will he not do? Hath he spoken, and will he not fulfil?" (Numbers 23:19). "We should not believe that God extends His mercy beyond the limits which He has revealed in Scripture" (St. Alphonsus Maria Liguori, "An Exposition and Defense of All Points of Faith Discussed and Defined by the Sacred Council of Trent," 140; Dublin: James Duffy & Co., 1846).

(5) Protestants worship the same God as we, don't they?

Protestantism has no worship of God. True worship of God consists of priest, altar, and sacrifice. Protestants rejected the priesthood, wanting no mediator between God and man. They have no consecrated altars. They cannot have the New Law sacrifice, which is Jesus Christ Himself, offered to the Father under the appearances of Bread and Wine, because only a properly ordained priest can produce this sacrifice, through Transubstantiation, on the altar. Pope Leo XIII solemnly assured us that Protestant-Anglican Orders were invalid. (The Bull "Apostolicae Curae," September 18, 1896).

(6) How is it, because of the infinite goodness of God, that none shall be saved without the true Faith of Jesus Christ, and without being in the communion of His Church, since by this means by far the greatest part of mankind must be lost – seeing that the number of those who have not the

faith and are not in the communion of His Church has always greatly exceeded the number of those who are?

The difficulty of reconciling this with the goodness of God, will easily vanish, and the goodness of God appear in all its beauty, if we consider what the Christian revelation teaches us concerning this matter. For here we learn that man, by the voluntary abuse of his free-will, having lost that happy state in which God, out of pure goodness, had created him, had rendered himself totally unworthy of any favour or mercy from God; so that God, without any breach of justice, nay, with the greatest justice, could, if He pleased, have left him without remedy, a prey to that misery which his sins deserved, as He actually did with the fallen angels. It was, therefore, the effect of His infinite goodness alone, that God was willing to show mercy to man at all; and still more so, that He was pleased to provide so unheard of a remedy for his evils as He did. "God so loved the world that He gave His only begotten Son," to seek and save those that were lost, by dying upon a cross for them. But as man, by the voluntary abuse of his free will, had lost the favour of God, God positively decreed that none who came to the full use of their reason, should reap the benefit of the redemption of Christ but by a voluntary performance of those conditions which He requires from them; for Christ is become "the cause of eternal salvation *to all that obey Him*" (Hebrews 5:9). And whereas man, by the miserable corruption of his nature by sin, was absolutely incapable of performing these conditions of himself; therefore God, out of the boundless riches of His goodness, and the sincere desire He has that all should be saved, through the merits of Jesus Christ, gives to all mankind, in whatever state or condition they be, such supernatural helps of His grace, as He sees proper for their present state, with a view to their salvation; that is to say, by these graces He moves them, and enables them to avoid some present evil, with this view, that, if they cooperate with this heavenly motion of His grace, He will give them more and greater graces; and if they continue their correspondence to those, He will go on to give them still more, till He bring them to the true

Faith and Church of Jesus Christ, and to a happy end; but, if they resist His graces, if they abuse them, and act contrary to them, if they reject these calls and offers of mercy which God gives them. . . , God, out of His infinite goodness, bears with them for a while, till at length He stops the continuation of such undeserved favours to them, and leaves them to perish in their own obstinacy and ingratitude. Hence, if the greater part of mankind is lost, this is wholly owing to themselves in abusing the goodness of God, and resisting the means He uses for their salvation; so that our salvation is only from the goodness of God, and our perdition wholly from ourselves, according to what He says by His prophet, "Destruction is thine, O Israel; thy help is only in Me" (Osee 13:9); "The grace of God our Saviour hath appeared to *all* men" (Ephesians 4:7); "He is the true light, which enlighteneth *every man* that cometh into this world" (John 1:9). The Holy Apostle Paul exhorts us "with fear and trembling to work out our salvation, for it is God that worketh in us, both to *will* and to *accomplish,* according to His good will" (Phillipians 2:12-13), showing that God will not be wanting if we do our part, and work according to the graces He gives us.

If the obstinacy of those outside the Church still increases and they go on shutting their eyes against the light of truth which God offers them, He then permits them to be seduced by falsehood to "give heed to spirits of error and doctrines of devils" (1 Tim 4:1). Thus, "because they received not the love of truth, that they might be saved; therefore God shall send them the operation of error, to believe lying, that all may be judged who have not believed the truth, but have consented to iniquity" (2 Thess. 2:10-11). This strong text clearly shows two great truths; first, that God gives to *all* the offers of the truth; and secondly, that the source of their damnation is entirely from *themselves,* in refusing to receive the truth. If, therefore, they still continue in their perversity, and die in their sin, a dreadful condemnation shall be their portion forever. ". . . when the Lord Jesus shall be revealed from Heaven, with the angels of His power: in a flame of fire, giving vengeance to them that *know not God,* and *who obey not the gospel of our Lord Jesus Christ"* (2 Thess. 1:8). To them "God swears in His wrath that they shall not enter into His rest" (Psalms 94:11). These are they who, having been invited to the marriage supper of the great King, rejected His invitation.

"The hand of the Lord is not shortened, that He cannot save," in whatever difficulties a poor soul may be. He has a thousand ways in His wisdom to conduct souls who are truly serious to the knowledge of the truth and to salvation. And though such a soul be in the remotest wilds of the world, God could be in no difficulty to send a Philip to him, or an angel from Heaven to instruct him (See Acts of the Apostles 8:26), for "God wills *all* men to be saved and to come to the knowledge of the truth" (1 Tim. 2:4).

(7)   Is it not an uncharitable doctrine to say that none can be saved outside the Catholic Church?

"If you love me, *keep my commandments,"* (John 14:15) stated our Blessed Lord. This is real charity, that we keep Christ's doctrine. Who shall dare say that a doctrine taught and declared by the great God is uncharitable? God is certainly at full liberty to require what conditions He pleases for bestowing His gifts upon us. Now, the whole tenor of His revealed will declares to us that He requires our being members of His Church, and our having the true faith of Jesus Christ, as indispensable conditions of salvation; and who shall dare find fault with Him for doing so?

The Catholic Church considers it as the height of charity to warn men of their danger in an affair of so immense importance as is that of their eternal salvation, and with the most tender compassion for their situation, uses every means in her power that they may be brought to the knowledge of the truth and be saved. *This* is true charity. For Charity is a virtue of the heart, which makes a man love his neighbor's *soul,* and to endeavor to promote his *salvation.* It is the man who is careless and indifferent about his neighbor's soul who deserves to be called uncharitable. It is plain, therefore, that the charge of being uncharitable is nothing but a malicious misrepresentation, and gross slander, invented only to render hateful the Catholic Church and her doctrine.

It would be an unkind thing to tell non-Catholics that they cannot be saved outside the Catholic Church if they could do nothing about it. That is, if it were impossible for them to become Catholics, or if becoming Catholics meant for them the forfeiting of something fine, noble, certain, and sustaining in their belief. Or if it meant the toppling over of beautiful dogmas; if a great edifice of belief had to go down in the face of our onslaught. But when we say there is no salvation outside the Catholic Church, we are being kind. We are saying "Come into the Ark. Here is your only salvation!"

But, you say, it seems so heartless to say there is no salvation outside the Catholic Church to one whom we know has close relatives who have died outside the Church. What about such a person's peace of mind? To that we answer: What about such a person's *soul?* Unless he believes this dogma he will not save his *own* soul! And what about the souls God has entrusted to his care – children, perhaps? All doctrines of the Catholic Church must be believed in order to gain our salvation. One cannot chose one and discard another. "Whosoever shall keep the whole law, but offend in *one* point, is become guilty of *all*" (James 2:10).

St. Francis Xavier, the great apostle to India and Japan, strongly preached the doctrine of no salvation outside the Catholic Church. The fruit of his uncompromising stand is the incredible number of his conversions. He was responsible for bringing *three million souls* into the Faith! On the other hand, the fruit of the liberal answer in our day to the question on salvation is that we are on the verge of the collapse of the Faith, and the collapse of our whole civilization which was built on that Faith. One of Our Lord's chief mercies to us, in this the most decadent era of our existence, is the message about where salvation is to be found. And the world, which is so miserably unhappy now, will but grow more so unless men accept this truth of Jesus Christ and *live* by it.

The crowning disloyalty to God is heresy. It is the sin of sins, the very loathsomest of things which God looks down upon in His world. Yet, how little do we understand of its excessive hatefulness. It is the polluting of God's Truth, which is the worst of all impurities. Yet how light we make of it. We look at it and are calm. We touch it and do not shudder. We mix with it and have no fear. We see it touch holy things, and we have no sense of sacrilege. We breathe its odor, and show no signs of detestation or disgust. Some of us even affect its friendship; and some even extenuate its guilt. *We do not love God enough to be angry for His glory. We do not love men enough to be charitably truthful for their souls.* Having lost the touch, the taste, the sight and all the senses of Heavenly-mindedness, we can dwell amidst this odious plague in imperturbable tranquility, reconciled to its foulness, not without some boastful profession of liberal admiration, perhaps even with a solicitous show of tolerant sympathies. Why are we so far below the old saints in the abundance of our conversions? Because we lack their ancient sternness. We lack the old Church spirit, the old ecclesiastical genius. Our charity is untruthful, because it is not severe; *and it is unpersuasive, because it is untruthful!* We lack devotion to truth as truth – as God's Truth. Our zeal for souls is puny, because we have no zeal for God's honor. We act as though God were complimented by conversions. We tell men half the truth, the half that best suits our own pusillanimity and their conceit; and then we wonder that so few are converted, and that of those few, so many apostatize. We are so weak as to be surprised that our half truths have not succeeded so well as God's whole truth. Where there is no hatred of heresy, there can be no holiness. A man who might be an apostle becomes a festering ulcer on the Body of the Church, for lack of this righteous indignation against the lie of the devil. We need St. Michael to put new hearts into us in these days of universal heresy!

(8) But, if a man acts according to the dictates of his conscience, and follows exactly the light of reason which God has implanted in him for his guide, is that not enough for him to be saved?

Not by itself, but if a man is *faithful* to his conscience, it will invariably lead him to join the Roman Catholic Church, which will then see to his salvation. But that a man's own conscience and reason can lead him to Heaven without the Church is, indeed, a specious proposition, and a great mistake lurks beneath it. When man was first created, his reason was *then* an enlightened reason. Illuminated by the grace of original righteousness, with which his soul was adorned, reason and conscience were then sure guides to conduct him in the way of salvation, but by sin this light was miserably darkened, and his reason became a prey to ignorance and error. It was not, indeed, entirely extinguished: it still teaches him many great things with regard to his conduct, but is at present so apt to be led astray by pride, passion, prejudice, and other such corrupt motives, that in numberless instances, it serves only to confirm him in his error, by giving appearance of reason to the suggestions of self-love and passion. And this is all too commonly the case, even in natural things. But in regard to supernatural things, concerning God and eternity, if left to itself our reason is virtually blind. To remedy this misery, God has given us the light of faith, as a sure and certain guide to conduct us to salvation, and has appointed His Holy Church as the guardian and depository of this heavenly light. Consequently, though a man pretends to act according to reason and conscience, and even flatters himself that he does so in things that regard his soul; yet if this reason and conscience be not enlightened and guided by the light of *true* faith, it can never lead him to salvation.

Nothing can be more striking than what the Holy Scripture says about this: "There is a way," says the wise man, "that *seemeth* right to a man, but the ends thereof lead to death" (Proverbs 14:12; and 16:25). And do not all those who are seduced by false prophets and false teachers *think* they are in the right way, and yet, in fact, running on the road to perdition? Is it not under the pretext of acting according to conscience that they are seduced? And yet the mouth of truth itself, Jesus Christ, expressly declared to his apostles, "The hour cometh, that whosoever killeth you, will think that he doth God a service" (John 16:2). But observe what He adds, "And these things will they do, *because they have not known the Father nor Me*" (Verse 3).

All the various religions which have been separated from the true Church in every age have uniformly and constantly calumniated and slandered her, and spoken evil of the way of truth professed by her, and were persuaded in their faulty and erroneous consciences that it was lawful and meritorious to do so. Will calumnies and slander against the Spouse of Jesus Christ save them, just because their conscience seems to approve them? Conscience tells a heathen that it is not only lawful, but a duty to worship idols, practice cannibalism and head-hunting. Will his acting in this manner, according to his conscience, save him? Or will these acts of idolatry be innocent and agreeable in the sight of God because they were performed according to conscience? Scripture says, "The idol that is made by hands is cursed, *as well as he that made it;* for that which is made, together with him that made it, shall suffer torments" (Wisdom 14:8-10). And, "To God, the wicked and his wickedness is hateful alike" (Wisdom 14:9).

(9) How is it that today many who profess themselves to be members of the Catholic Church call this truth into question themselves by continually pleading in favor of those who are not of their communion, proposing excuses for them, and using all their endeavors to prove the possibility of salvation for those who live and die in a false religion?

This is one of those infernal heresies which the enemy of souls makes use of in these unhappy times to promote his own cause, and which has found its way even among those who profess to be of the fold of Christ. For, as they live among those who are of another communion, and often have the most intimate connections with them, they contact a natural love and a sensual affection for them. This makes them, first, sorry to think their friends should be out of the way of salvation. Then they proceed to wish and hope they may not be so. Hence they come to call into question if they be so; and from this step it is easy to grasp at every pretext to persuade themselves they are not so. Lax principles are everywhere present in these our days; uncovenanted tolerance is found to be in God for Turks, Jews, and Infidels, which had never before been heard of among Christians. This is gilded over with the specious character of a liberal way of thinking and generous sentiments; and it has become the fashion to think and speak in this manner. Now, fashion is a most powerful persuasive, which even good people are not always proof against; and, when one hears these sentiments every day resounding in his ears, and anything that seems contrary to them ridiculed and condemned, this naturally clouds the understanding, and discourages the mind from so much as *wishing* to examine the strength of these sentiments, for fear of finding out their falsehood. When, for fear of being despised, we wish error to be true, it is very easy to believe it to be true; and every sophistical show of reason in its favour is adopted, without further examination, as conclusive. Worldly interest also very often concurs, with its overbearing influence, to produce the same end. A member of the Catholic Church has relatives or friends who never have been members of the Church, or who have left the Church. The thought that they are outside salvation pains him. He therefore begins to wish they could be saved as they are, in their own religion. Hence he comes to doubt but that they may be saved, and gladly adopts any show of "proof" to make him think that they will be. It is true, indeed, that none of these reasons would influence a member of the Catholic Church who holds his faith sincerely, and who has a knowledge of what it teaches him on this subject in her official magisterium – not in her individual members who have no guarantee from Christ to be preserved from error. Only Peter, speaking through the popes ex cathedra, has that promise. (As we said earlier, the great heresies in the history of the Catholic Church came mainly from her priests who had lost the faith, or who had stealthily entered into the Church to weaken and destroy it under cover of "sheep's clothing"). But the great misfortune of many who give in to these loose ways of thinking and speaking is that they are ignorant of the grounds of their religion. They do not examine the matter to the bottom; and if once they begin to be infected by the spirit of the day, they are unwilling to examine it. They even take it amiss if any zealous friend should attempt to *undeceive* them. And grasping at these miserable sophisms, which are alleged in favor of their loose way of thinking, they refuse to open their eyes to the truth, or even to look at the arguments which support it.

When those outside the Church see the members of the Church talking dubiously on this head, what can they think? Must it not unavoidably tend to lull them to sleep, to extinguish any desire of inquiry after the truth?

If once a Catholic begins to doubt the necessity of his Faith, what esteem can he have for the laws, rules, or practice of it? Self-love, always attentive to its own satisfaction, will soon tell him that, if it be not absolutely necessary to be of that religion (in order to be saved), much less necessary must it be to submit to all its regulations; hence liberties are taken in practice, inconsistent with their duty, the commands of the Church are despised, the exercises of devotion neglected, and a shadow of religion introduced under the show of liberal sentiments, but to the destruction of solid virtue and piety. *(Is it not crystal clear what is happening in the Catholic Church today, and the reason for it?)*

(10) How can the people know when their Bishops and Priests are teaching them error?

Just as no man would deny that he is responsible for his own salvation, so also would he not deny that God has given him equipment enough for knowing when he has heard the truth and when he has not. God's grace is not lacking to anyone who will accept it, and the mind is made for *truth,* not for error. (He "enlighteneth *every* man that cometh into this world" – John 1-9). Every Catholic knows, for instance, that when a Jewish rabbi, who denies the divinity of Christ, and a Protestant minister, who doubts it, get on a stage with a Catholic priest, who agrees to forget it for the evening (in the interest of mutual brotherhood), something is wrong. In the Catholic's heart of hearts he knows it. And that knowledge makes every Catholic responsible. Christ, carrying His cross, did not say to the women of Jerusalem when He met them bewailing and lamenting Him: "Daughters of Jerusalem, weep for the high priest and the priests who have let this awful thing be done, and have despoiled you of your spiritual heritage." Rather, He said to them: "Daughters of Jerusalem, weep not over me; but weep for yourselves, and for your children" (Luke 23:28).

(11) A person has only himself to blame for remaining outside the Church.

Let us remember that it is *of the Faith* that God wills all men to be saved: "Who will have all men to be saved and to come to the knowledge of the truth" (1 Timothy 2:4). God, because He wills all men to be saved, gives every man the graces necessary to help him achieve his salvation through Christ and His Church. It is God's command that all men be saved through the Catholic Church. St. John Chrysostom says, "It is not lawful to say 'I cannot' for that means you are accusing the Creator. For if He made us incapable and yet gives us commands, the fault lies with *Him.* Whence it comes, then you will say, that so many 'cannot'? *Because they will not.* How then is it that they will not? Through *sloth,* for if they would but will, they would be quite capable. For we have God to help and assist us, let us only choose, only approach it as a task, only be anxious to apply our minds to it, and all things follow."

It is also typical of liberal Catholics that seeing some men without the Faith, *they blame it on God,* Who would withhold His 'gift of Faith' from such men, rather than on the bad will and slothfulness of these men. If Faith is a gift, no man can have it who refuses it when it is offered to him, or who does not ardently desire it when far from it. The reason then why so many men have not the 'gift of Faith' is because *they will not take it!* It is true to say that they 'cannot' believe, but this is only because they 'will not.' Consequently, according to His Sacred Covenant, God also 'will not' save them – unless before they die they become members of His Church.

The Doctors of the Church bring out that when God does withhold the Catholic Faith from a person, it is only because that person is unworthy of it, and has not responded to the other graces already given to him.

A man can be blamed even for not having desired to hear of Christ, for had he sought fervently, and followed the guidance of his natural reason, God would have sent him some preacher of the Faith, as He sent St. Peter to Cornelius. (Acts of the Apostles, Chap. 10). God, in His Mercy, cannot refuse the grace of the Catholic Faith to a man who earnestly desires it, for it is God Himself Who places this desire in his heart. It is completely against God's Justice and Mercy to affirm that some good and sincere people can be found to whom God would refuse His truth and His graces. No greater lack of charity can be found than to make such a statement.

(12) What about "invincible ignorance"?

A man who lives, let us say, in the United States, knows that it is a governed nation. He knows that this government was established for his good, and indispensably so. He also knows that he must investigate with reasonable diligence its laws, because he must observe these laws, or else be punished for not doing so. There is no man who has not enough civic and social wisdom to get rid of his ignorance about the laws of his State. Likewise, a man looking around the world knows that the world is governed by God. And with Christian challenges staring him in the face and shouting into his ears, he must know that this world is governed by Christ, true God and true Man. If he is to save his soul, he knows that he must investigate what are the laws of this government of Christ. And it should be evident to him that the rules laid down for his salvation by Jesus Christ cannot possibly be found in those Christian churches which speak without authority – and which disagree among themselves as to what the very rules might be.

It could happen, with regard to a particular law, that the State might find an individual ignorant of it through no fault of his own. He would then be morally exonerated, but he would still be legally punished, because that is the law. For example, a man who did not know where he had to pay his income tax, and therefore avoided paying it, would not be excused for not having searched around until he had found out where to pay it. The officer of the law might sympathize with the man in his ignorance, but he would have to penalize him for not observing the law, or else it would be foolish for a State to make laws at all. If the State were to leave it to the sincerity of the citizens to imagine what civic laws should be – and then obey those they privately thought were for the public good – we would see the complete end of the common welfare, for which the State was instituted.

Christ laid down the law of salvation, and this law must be observed so as to secure salvation. Even the most liberal Catholic theologians must hold that no unbaptized baby can see God in the Beatific Vision, because he has not fulfilled the law laid down for such beatitude. He has never been baptized.

Well, you say, what about the native in the desert? See Acts of the Apostles, 8:26-39: God sent Philip down from Jerusalem into the Gaza desert to find a lone Ethiopian, a eunuch, in order to convert and baptize him. It is clear why God sent Philip on his long journey to the eunuch, because immediately after the baptism was administered, the Spirit of the Lord took Philip away. Every native of good will in the world will be found by some Catholic missionary if the native is willing to take the Faith! It is terribly surprising to find a soul who admits that his unbaptized baby who died at childbirth will never see God, but holds that some unbaptized native who lived a few more years in a much worse condition, will be saved! So, to repeat, if there is a native in the desert whom God knows is willing to receive the message of Christ, God will get him a missionary, just as He got Philip to the eunuch. If no missionary comes, *it will be because God sees no missionary would be received, were he to come!*

The "First Draft of the Dogmatic Constitution on the Church of Christ" at the Third Session of the First Vatican Council, on April 24th, 1870, which included the heresy of invincible ignorance, was never voted on by the Council Fathers, since it is not the authentic teaching of the Church. (See Collectio Lacensis, VII, 567 ff.) Invincible ignorance was introduced into Chapter 7. The Holy Ghost will never allow error in the *official magisterium.* The liberals tried to "sandwich" this error in, hoping that it would pass. It didn't.

<u>"Invincible Ignorance" is refuted by Scripture, the Councils, Doctors, and Saints of the Church:</u>

"God will have *all* men to be saved, *and to come to the knowledge of the truth"* (1 Tim. 2:4).

"If then God wills *all* to be saved, it follows that He gives to *all* that grace and those aids which are necessary for the attainment of salvation, otherwise it could never be said that He has a *true will* to save all. It is certain, in contradiction to the blasphemies of Luther and Calvin, that God does not impose a law that is impossible to be observed" (St. Alphonsus Maria de Liguori).

"God commands not impossibilities; but by commanding He suggests to you to do what you can, to ask for what is beyond your strength; and He helps you so that you may be able" (St. Augustine).

"The true light enlightens *every man* that cometh into the world" (John 1:9).

"But if anyone is not enlightened, this is the fault of the man who turns himself away from the light that would enlighten him" (St. Thomas Aquinas).

"Although no one is converted except he is drawn by the Father, yet let no one pretend to excuse himself on the plea of not being drawn. God stands at the gate and knocks by the internal and the external word" (Council of Cologne, A.D. 1536, Art. 32, Vid. Dict. Council et Migne). "Behold, I stand at the gate and knock. If any man will hear My voice, and open the door to Me, I will come in and sup with him" (Apocalypse 3:20).

"Everyone that asketh, receiveth, and he that seeketh findeth" (Luke 11:10).

(13) But, will not being good on a purely *natural* level obtain our salvation?

However corrupted our nature is by sin, yet all the children of Adam have some good natural dispositions, some being more inclined to one virtue, some to another. Thus some are of a humane benevolent disposition; some tender-hearted and compassionate towards others in distress; some just and upright in their dealings; some temperate and sober; some mild and patient; some have a natural turn to devotion, and a kind of respect for the Supreme Being. Now, all such good natural dispositions of themselves are far from being supernatural Christian virtues, and altogether incapable to bring a man to the supernatural life of Heaven. They, indeed, make him who has them agreeable to men, and procure him esteem and regard from those with whom he lives; but they are of no ultimate avail before God with regard to his eternal salvation. To be convinced of this we need only observe that good natural dispositions of this kind are found in Turks, Jews, and Heathens, as well as among Christians; yet no Christian can suppose that a Turk, Jew, or Heathen will obtain the kingdom of Heaven by means of these qualities.

No good works whatsoever, performed through the good dispositions of nature only, can ever be crowned by God with eternal happiness. To obtain this glorious reward, our good works must be sanctified by the blood of Jesus, and become *supernatural* works of Christian virtue, *performed in the state of sanctifying grace.* We must be united to Jesus Christ by *true* Faith (the Faith that comes to us from the Apostles), which is the root and foundation of all Christian virtues; for St. Paul expressly says, "Without Faith it is impossible to please God" (Hebrews 11:6). Hence it is manifest that those who die in a false religion, however exceptional their moral conduct may be in the eyes of men, yet as they lack the *true* Faith of Christ, and thus are not pleasing to Him, are not in the way of salvation. "One Lord, *one* Faith, one Baptism" (Eph. 4:5).

(14) Don't you think that you can win people to the True Faith more easily by not being so outspoken? Don't you think you can convert many more by *good example?*

What modern Catholics are doing under this good neighbor policy is to bring, not Jesus Christ, but *themselves* to those outside the Church. They are luring people into liking *them.* Whether Catholics are pleasant-mannered or un-pleasant-mannered is no ultimate proof that the Catholic Church is the one true Church. The Catholic Church is the one true Church because it was founded by Jesus Christ on His Apostles, with Peter and his successors as His Vicars and visible head, and with His promise that the gates of hell shall never prevail against it. We should never purposely try to frighten people off by a stern approach, of course, but we should likewise never fear to approach all men with the stern warnings and "hard sayings" of Jesus Christ. As Our Lord Himself said: "He that shall be ashamed of Me and of My words in this adulterous and sinful generation, of him will the Son of Man also be ashamed when He shall come in the glory of His Father with the holy angels" (Mark 8:38).

MODERNISM: THE TEMPTATION AGAINST FAITH

Modernism was noticed first among the younger clergy of Italy, exposed all their lives to liberal teachings. Pope St. Pius X attacked it as far back as 1887, when he was Bishop of Mantua and denounced "Modern Christianity," as it was then called. This "Modern Christianity" is an organized and methodic skepticism of thought in the matter of Scripture, Theology, and Church History, of the kind instituted in the early nineteenth century by Immanuel Kant, in philosophy. It earned the name "Modernism" on the ground that modern scholarship had not tested religious truths according to modern standards so as to determine their value! Pope St. Pius X called it "the synthesis and poison of all heresies which tend to undermine the fundamentals of the Faith and to annihilate Christianity," and it was especially heartbreaking to him since it affected the clergy, for whose purity of doctrine and holiness of life he had spent his greatest efforts. "We priests must grow in sanctity of life and purity of doctrine if people are to be formed in Christ," he said in his first encyclical; and later, in the apostolic letter "Scripturae Sanctae," he expressed his ardent desire to advance the study of Holy Scripture among the clergy, "especially in our time when the human intellect tries to overstep the boundaries of its own limitations and attack *the fountain of Divine Revelation."* Pope St. Pius X realized, with the clear-sightedness of a saint, that Modernism was nothing in reality but a rejection of all the dogmas of Faith, on the basis of the diabolical consideration that all truth is *relative,* and nothing absolutely true. It was the age-old rejection of Pilate all over again: "What is truth?"

Pope St. Pius X not only excoriated the Modernists for their teachings, but he undertook to smoke them out of the Church by the strongest of disciplines. He laid down a law requiring that no candidate could henceforth be admitted to the priesthood until he took an oath before his bishop against Modernism and all it stands for. He never ceased, during all of his pontificate, to express his horror and condemnation of the liberals as the polluters of Catholic doctrine and religious allegiances. He said of them, when he was Cardinal: "Catholic liberals are wolves in sheeps' clothing; hence any priest worthy of the name must unmask for the faithful confided to his care their insidious plotting, their unholy design. You shall be called papists, clericals, retrogressives, intransigents. *Be proud of it!"*

THE INTERFAITH MOVEMENT

Let us see what Holy Scripture and the Church teach about communicating in religion with those who are separated from us. The Right Reverend Archbishop George Hay in his book "The Sincere Christian," which was first published in 1787, states:

"Whoever seriously considers . . . the light in which the sacred scriptures represent to us all false religions will have no difficulty in drawing this conclusion: that every comunication with such, in religious matters, must be highly criminal in the sight of God; *because every such*

*communication implies an approbation of their false
doctrine,* and is, as St. John expresses it, a communicating
with their wicked works (2 John 11). In Holy Scripture, we
are assured that false religions arise from false teachers
who are called seducers of the people, ravenous wolves,
false prophets, who speak perverse things; that they are
antichrists, and enemies of the cross of Christ; that
departing from the true faith of Christ they give heed to
spirits of error; that their doctrines are doctrines of devils,
speaking lies; that their ways are pernicious, their heresies
damnable, and the like. In Consequence of which, this
general command of avoiding all communication with them
in religion is given by the apostle: 'Bear not the yoke
together with unbelievers; for what participation hath
justice with injustice? or what fellowship hath light with
darkness? And what concord hath Christ with Belial? or
what part hath the faithful with the unbelievers?' (2 Cor.
6:14). Now, it is the true religion of Jesus Christ, the true
doctrine of His Gospel, which is justice and light; all false
doctrines are injustice and darkness; . . . all false religions
flow from the father of lies, and make those who embrace
them unbelievers; therefore, all participation, all
fellowship, all communication with false religions, is here
expressly forbidden by *the word of God.* . . .We are obliged
to love the persons of those who are engaged in false
religions, to wish them well, and do them good; but here we
are expressly forbidden all communication in their
religion; that is, their false tenets and worship.

"The Spirit of Christ, which dictated the Holy Scriptures,
and the Spirit which animates and guides the Church of
Christ and teaches her all truth, is the same; and therefore
her conduct in this point has been uniformly the same in
all ages with what the Holy Scripture teaches. She has
constantly prohibited her children to have any
communication in religious matters with those who are
separated from her communion; and this she has
sometimes done under the most severe penalties. In the
apostolical canons, which are of very ancient standing, and
for the most part handed down from the apostolical age, it

is thus decreed: 'If any bishop, or priest, or deacon shall join in prayers with heretics, let him be suspended from communion.' (Canon 44). Also, 'If any clergyman, or layman shall go into the synagogue of the Jews, or the meetings of heretics, to join in prayer with them, let them be deposed, and deprived of communion.' (Canon 63). So also, in one of her most respectable councils, held in the year 398, at which the great St. Augustine was present, she speaks thus, 'None must either pray or sing psalms with heretics; and whosoever shall communicate with those who are cut off from the communion of the church, whether clergyman or layman, let him be excommunicated.' (Council of Carthage, IV. 72 & 73).

"See here whom we are to avoid: those who cause dissensions contrary to the old doctrine; all those who, having left the true faith and doctrine which they had learned, and which had been handed down to us from the beginning by the Church of Christ, follow strange doctrines, and make divisions and dissensions in the Christian world. And why are we to avoid them? Because they are not servants of Christ, but slaves to their own belly, whose hearts are placed upon the enjoyments of this world, and who, by 'pleasing speeches and good words, seduce the hearts of the innocent'; that is, do not bring any reasons or solid arguments to seduce people to their evil ways, so as to convince the understanding, for that is impossible; but practice upon their hearts and passions, relaxing the laws of the gospel; granting liberties to the inclinations of flesh and blood, laying aside the sacred rules of mortification of the passions, and of self-denial, promising worldly wealth, and ease, and honors, and, by pleasing speeches of this kind, seducing the heart and engaging people to their ways.

"The same argument and command the apostle repeats in his epistle to his beloved disciple Timothy, where he gives a sad picture, indeed, of all false teachers, and, withal, tells us, that they put on an outward show of piety, the better to deceive, 'having an appearance, indeed, of godliness, but denying the power thereof'; then he immediately gives this command: 'Now, these avoid: for, of this sort are they that creep into houses, and lead captive silly women laden with sins, who are led away with diverse desires'; and adds this sign by which they may be known, that, not having the true faith of Christ, and being out of his holy church, *the only sure rule for knowing the truth,* they are never settled, but are always altering and changing their opinions, 'ever learning, and never attaining to the knowledge of the truth'; and no wonder, because as he adds: 'they resist the truth, being corrupted in their mind, and reprobate concerning the faith' (2 Tim. 3:5-8). Here it is to be observed, that, though the apostle says that silly weak peopie, and especially women, are most apt to be deceived by such false teachers, yet he gives the command of avoiding all communication with them in their evil ways, to all without exception, even to Timothy himself, for the epistle is directed particularly to him, and to him he says, as well as to all others, 'Now these avoid,' though he was a pastor of the church, and fully instructed by the apostle himself in all the truths of religion; because, besides the danger of seduction, which none can escape who voluntarily expose themselves to it, *all such communication is evil in itself,* and therefore to be avoided by all, and especially by pastors, whose example would be more prejudicial to others.

"Lastly, the beloved disciple St. John renews the same command in the strongest terms, and adds another reason, which regards all without exception, and especially those who are best instructed in their duty: 'Look to yourselves,' says he, 'that ye lose not the things that ye have wrought, but that ye may receive a full reward. Whosoever revolteth and continueth not in the doctrine of Christ, hath not God' (2 John 8,9). Wherefore, whatever arguments may be brought from . . . wordly motives, from interest, gaining favor, liberality of sentiment, sociality, curiosity, levity, gayety, or the like, to induce us to join in, or partake of any religious duty with those of a false religion, though but in appearance only, let us look upon all such arguments as vain deceit and worldly wisdom: and let us oppose to all such reasons, this one argument: *God has expressly forbidden it; therefore no human power can make it lawful!"*

Have the Fathers of the Church Had Anything to Say on This Subject?

St. Cyprian (d. 258), in the Footnotes of the Fathers of the Church on Chapter 16 of the Book of Numbers, of Holy Scripture, states: "We are warned to keep in the true Church, and to obey those who are set over us; and never, *for any temporal considerations whatever,* to encourage by our presence, the sermons or meetings of heretics, or of schismatics, lest we perish with them. . . If we give any encouragement to schismatics, or go to their meetings, *we must expect to be involved in their sins."*

Have the Popes Spoken, Officially, on This Subject?

On January 6, 1928 Pope Pius XI issued the encyclical "Mortalium Animos" ("Fostering True Religious Unity"). In it he states:

"When there is a question of fostering unity among Christians, it is easy for many to be misled by the apparent excellence of the object to be achieved. Is it not right, they ask, is it not the obvious duty of all who invoke the name of Christ to refrain from mutual reproaches and at last to be united in charity?

"Those . . . who strive for the union of the Churches would appear to pursue the noblest of ideals in promoting charity among all Christians. But how would charity tend to the detriment of Faith? Everyone knows that John himself, the Apostle of love, who seems in his Gospel to have revealed the secrets of the Sacred Heart of Jesus, and who never ceased to impress upon the memory of his disciples the new Commandment 'to love one another,' nevertheless strictly forbade any intercourse with those who professed a mutilated and corrupt form of Christ's doctrine: 'If any man come to you, and bring not this doctrine, receive him not into the house, nor say to him, God speed you' (2 John 10).

"This Apostolic See has never allowed its subjects to take part in the assemblies of non-Catholics. There is but one way in which the unity of Christians may be fostered, and that is by furthering the return to the one true Church of Christ of those who are separated from it; for from that one true Church they have in the past fallen away. The one Church of Christ is visible to all, and will remain, according to the Will of its Author, exactly the same as He instituted it. . . Since the Mystical Body of Christ (The Roman Catholic Church), like His physical body, is *one* (I Cor. 12:12), compactly and fitly joined together (Eph. 4:15-16), it would be foolish to say that the Mystical Body is composed of disjointed and scattered members. Whosoever therefore is not united with the body is no member thereof, neither is he in communion with Christ its head.

"Furthermore, in this one Church of Christ no man can be or remain who does not accept, recognize, and obey the authority and supremacy of Peter and his legitimate successors.

"Let our separated children, therefore, draw nigh to the Apostolic See, set up in the City which Peter and Paul, Princes of the Apostles, consecrated by their blood; . . . and let them come, not with any intention or hope that 'the Church of the living God, the pillar and ground of the truth' (I Tim. 3:15), will cast aside the integrity of the faith and tolerate their errors, but to submit themselves to its teaching and government."

WHAT IS MEANT BY THE WORDS
"RELIGIOUS LIBERTY"?

Religious liberty does not mean the right to believe anything one desires. It means, rather, freedom from restraint in forming a good conscience and in believing what one ought to believe. It is the freedom ultimately to obey the laws of God as laid down in Divine Revelation and as interpreted by His Vicar, His voice on earth, the Holy Roman Pontiff.

Here is a true story from the life of the Cure' of Ars – St. John Marie Vianney: The Cure' of Ars once gave a medal to a Protestant who visited him, who exclaimed, "Dear Sir, you have given a medal to one who is a heretic, at least I am a heretic from your point of view. But although we are not of the same religion, I hope we shall both one day be in Heaven." The holy priest took the gentleman's hand in his own, and giving him a look which seemed to reach his very soul, answered him, "Alas! my friend, we cannot be together in Heaven, unless we have begun to live so in this world. Death makes no change in that. As the tree falls so shall it lie. Jesus Christ has said, 'He that does not hear the Church, let him be to thee as a heathen and a publican.' And He said again, 'There shall be one fold and one shepherd,' and He made St. Peter the chief shepherd of His flock." Then, in a voice full of sweetness, he added, "My dear friend, there are not *two ways* of serving Jesus Christ; there is only *one* way, and that is to serve Him as He Himself wishes to be served." Saying this, the priest left him. But these words sank deeply into the good man's heart, and led him to renounce the errors into which he had fallen, and he became a fervent Catholic.

Before leaving the subject of Where Salvation is to be Found, I would like to say a few words about the late Father Leonard Feeney, a Jesuit priest in the United States who, back in 1949, publicly defended and fought for the absolute truth of the doctrine of no salvation outside the Catholic Church. Certain censures were placed on him for doing so, and he was dismissed from the Jesuit Order. His followers were the members of St. Benedict Center, a Catholic lay organization in Cambridge, Massachusetts, founded for the purpose of encouraging the life of the Church among the people of Cambridge and particularly the students of Harvard University and Radcliffe College. Father Feeney was their spiritual director.

Here is a personal letter Father Feeney wrote to His Holiness, Pope Pius XII, on May 28, 1949:

"It is with the deepest anguish that I write to You, the Vicar of Christ on earth, to ask you to protect me in the crusade which God has given me to wage in Your defense and in the defense of our Holy Faith in the United States of America. . .

"Your Holiness must believe me when I tell You that the condition of the Church in the United States of America in the matter of doctrine is utterly deplorable. There is no doubt about it that we are slowly becoming a National Church, controlled not in the least by Your Holiness, but by the National Catholic Welfare Council of Washington, D.C. Americans are not being taught the Catholic Faith as it is contained in the writings of the Fathers and the Doctors and in the definitions of the Councils of the Church. They are being taught what a committee of extremely deficient American theologians thinks will interest the American mind without ever embarrassing or challenging it.

"I am writing this letter to Your Holiness simply, and as a child. Your Holiness may see already that it is not a legally organized document. It is a cry of anguish from my priestly heart. In order not to tire you with too many details, may I tell you in brief statement what is the fundamental heresy universally taught by Catholics, priests and teachers, in the United States of America. This is the doctrine which American Catholics are being taught: 'The way to be saved is by being sincere to your convictions and living a good life. If one of your convictions happens to be that the

Roman Catholic Church is the true Church of Christ, then you are obliged to join it. If you do not sincerely think it is the one way to salvation, then you are invincibly ignorant and God will save you, apart from the Church. You are then said to belong to the soul of the Church, and whatever you desire for yourself in the way of salvation, Catholic theologians are prepared to call 'Baptism of Desire.' Were you to sincerely think that the Roman Catholic Church is not the true Church of Christ, it would be a sin for you to join it.'

"Your Holiness, I assure You in all my honour, in the sanctity of my Sacrament and whatever voice I have to be heard in profession of Faith, that the above statement is the substance of what is being taught all Americans as the means of eternal salvation. I am bold enough to say that you know what I am telling You is the truth. There is no Pope in history who has been as close to the American mind as you have been. . . Every day that you defer calling a halt to the wild Liberalism of the American hierarchy, a Liberalism which pays not the slightest attention to Your messages against Interfaith movements and against exposing our Catholics to the dangers of heretical perversion, the more will grow the spirit of indifference and apostasy in our land, and ten years from now will be too late to save it. I know that along with this challenge which I offer to Your Holiness, while prostrate at Your feet in reverence and love, there go thousands of graces to enable You as Christ's Vicar to save this world for our Holy Faith. . ."

Father Feeney did not receive a personal reply from the Holy Father, but in August, 1950 the Pope came out with the encyclical "Humani Generis" in which he condemned those who "reduce to a meaningless formula the necessity of belonging to the True Church in order to gain salvation." Then in 1972 Pope Paul VI lifted all ecclesiastical censures on Father Feeney and, later, on members of St. Benedict Center, *without asking that they recant one iota of the doctrine which supposedly had incurred those censures in*

1949! Since a heretic can never be reinstated without a formal renunciation of his errors, this action of Pope Paul VI proved conclusively that Father Feeney and his followers had never been in error on this point!

WILL ALL CATHOLICS BE SAVED?

No! It is not enough to be a Catholic to get to Heaven. One has to be a *good* Catholic. "Many Catholics will be lost, because they are only nominal, not practical, Catholics, and because they reject some doctrines of the Catholic Church, especially such as oppose their inclinations and passions. Remember, he who rejects even *one* doctrine proposed to our Faith by the Church will certainly be lost (James 2:10), even though he should lead a good life." (From THE PULPIT ORATOR, Volume VI.)

Our Lord said, "He who believes shall be saved" (Mark 16:16). But God said many other things as well:

"If you love me, keep my commandments" (John 14:15); and "If thou wilt enter into life, keep the commandments" (Matt. 19:17).

"He that blasphemeth the name of the Lord, dying let him die" (Lev. 24:16).

"Keep you my Sabbath: for it is holy unto you. He that shall profane it, shall be put to death. Everyone that shall do any work on this day shall die" (Exodus 31:14-15).

"Know you not that the unjust shall not possess the kingdom of God? Do not err: neither idolaters, nor thieves, nor covetous, nor drunkards, nor railers, nor extortioners, shall possess the kingdom of God" (1 Cor. 6:9-10).

"A thief is better than a man that is always lying: but both of them shall inherit destruction" (Ecclus. 20:27).

"Neither fornicators nor adulterers . . . shall possess the kingdom of God" (1 Cor. 6:9). "Keep thyself chaste" (1 Tim. 5:22). "Blessed are the clean of heart for *they* shall see God" (Matt. 5:8).

"There is not a more wicked thing than to love money, for such a one setteth even his own soul at stake . . . " (Ecclus. 10:10).

"If anyone lie with a man as with a woman, both have committed an abomination. Let them be put to death" (Lev. 20:13).

"Hear me, and I will show thee who they are, over whom the devil can prevail. For they who in such manner receive matrimony, as to shut out God from themselves, and from their mind, and to give themselves to their lust, as the horse and mule, which have not understanding, over them the devil has power" (Book of Tobias, 6:16-22).

And Christ's Mystical Body on earth, His Church ("He who hears you, hears Me" – Luke 10:16), says:

"Each act of marriage must be left open to conception" (Pope Pius XI's Encyclical "Casti Connubi", December 31, 1930).

"If anyone says that the commandments of God are, even for one that is justified and constituted in grace, impossible to observe, let him be anathema" (Council of Trent, Canon 18 on Justification).

"If anyone says that a man who is justified and however perfect is not bound to observe the commandments of God *and the Church,* but only to believe, as though the Gospel were a bare and absolute promise of eternal life without the condition of obeying the commandments, let him be anathema" (Council of Trent, Canon 20 on Justification).

Therefore, although it is true that Catholics alone profess the true faith "without which," as St. Paul assures us, "it is impossible to please God" (Heb. 11:6); nevertheless, as St. James concludes: "Faith, without good works, is dead" (James 1:22:27).

"Sometimes people say 'It is better to be a good Protestant than a bad Catholic.' That is not true. That would mean at bottom that one could be saved without the true Faith. No, a bad Catholic remains a child of the family – although a prodigal; and however great a sinner he may be, he still has the right to mercy. Through his faith, a bad Catholic is nearer to God than a Protestant is, for he is a member of the household, whereas the Protestant is not. And how hard it is to make him become one!" (St. Peter Julian Eymard, 1811-1868).

GOD'S MERCY AND JUSTICE

"If the wicked do penance for all his sins which he hath committed and keep all my commandments and do judgment and justice, living he shall live, and shall not die. I will not remember all his iniquities that he hath done: in his justice which he hath wrought, he shall live. Is it my will that a sinner should die, saith the Lord God, and not that he should be converted from his ways and live?

"And you have said: The way of the Lord is not right. Hear ye, therefore. . . Is it *my* way that is not right, and are not rather *your* ways perverse?

"Therefore will I judge every man according to his ways . . . saith the Lord God. Be converted, and do penance for all your iniquities: and iniquity shall not be your ruin. Cast away from you all your transgressions, by which you have transgressed, and make to yourselves a new heart and a new spirit" (Ezechiel, Chapter 18), for "Wisdom will not dwell in a body subject to sins" (Wisdom 1:4).

TO OBTAIN SALVATION IS THE PURPOSE OF LIFE!

This whole world was made by God from the very beginning to be a world in which *salvation* is the greatest challenge. Our Lord told His Apostles: "Go forth and teach all nations." Tell them what they should be *looking for!* The one effort which a man ought to be making every moment of his life is toward the saving of his immortal soul. Everything else would take care of itself – sanity, certitude, vocation, employment, marriage, children – all would be beautifully taken care of, if the saving of his immortal soul were the first aim of every man. "Seek ye first the kingdom of God and His justice, and all these things shall be added unto you" (Luke 12:31).

WE HAVE HERE "NO ABIDING CITY" (From Lenten Conferences given by Father Bede Jarrett, O.P., at Our Lady of Victories, Kensington, England, 1932).

"We are pilgrims – travelers; we have no lasting city here; we have no home. We are urged to live, remembering that we are travellers. This will help you to explain your life to yourself. As you look at your life, perhaps it seems unsatisfactory. It has no apparent continual growth in an orderly progressive fashion. True, for life is not really a growing up, but a journey. You are a traveller rather than a growing child. You are taking a journey to life eternal. People are disappointed because they do not understand this.

"We are always planning and designing for ourselves what one day we shall do. As children we planned what we were to do when we had grown up. In youth we planned for our middle years. As we grow older it is always in the future that the great event, whatever it is, is to happen. We plan, at last, to settle down in old age. We cannot settle down. We never shall. We are *pilgrims!* . . .If you are to go on a long pilgrimage you must accommodate yourself to others. So life is an endless accommodating of ourselves to others.

You say when you begin: 'This is only for a short time; later on I shall be able to organize my life as I want it.' That will happen truly, but not *here*. No one here ever really has a chance of having exactly what he wants. Only on the other side will you really have a home. We belong to a great city, but the city lies over the far side of the river. So live that you remember whence you came, and whither you journey. Keep your eyes steadily fixed on the height towards which you climb. . . .Forget the things that are behind you. . . .Strive earnestly forward. . . .Nothing here on earth can ever content us. We get past one difficulty only to encounter another. That is right and proper. Indeed, that is life! So do not expect to find here your city – the thing perfectly worked out, complete, that you desire, dream of, work for. Do not expect to be able to settle down for long to enjoy your life. The danger that assaults us is the danger that we might settle down. We are pilgrims on the march. Always beware of comfort! Beware of being content with what you have! There – ahead – is your comfort. Pilgrims, travellers, strangers, that is all we be! We seek a city, whose maker and builder is *God,* a city that is *God Himself.* We shall enter within it by His mercy. God Himself shall be our home. Cannot you be grateful for the road, though it be rough? It does all a road was ever made to do. It takes you *home!*"

With much love, and many prayers that you will come back home to our Mother – the Holy, Roman, Catholic Church.

Your friend.

REFERENCES

HOLY SCRIPTURE, Douay-Rheims Translation

THE CHURCH TEACHES: Documents of the Church in English Translation by Jesuit Fathers of St. Mary's College, St. Mary's, Kansas

THE TEACHINGS OF THE CHURCH FATHERS, edited by John R. Willis, S.J.

THE CHURCH: Papal Teachings, selected and arranged by the Benedictine Monks of Solesmes

CATECHISM OF THE COUNCIL OF TRENT, Translated by Fathers McHugh and Callan

HANDBOOK OF THE CHRISTIAN RELIGION, Fr. W. Wilmers, S.J.

APOLOGETICS AND CATHOLIC DOCTRINE, by the Most Rev. M. Sheehan, D.D.

THE SUNDAY SERMONS OF THE GREAT FATHERS, translated and edited by Fr. M. F. Toal, D.D.

THE LITURGICAL YEAR, by Abbot Dom Gueranger, O.S.B.

THE SINCERE CHRISTIAN, by Rt. Rev. Bishop Hay

FAITHS FOR THE FEW: A Study of Minority Religions, by Wm. Whalen

THE LOYOLAS AND THE CABOTS, by Slaves of the Immaculate Heart of Mary, Still River, Mass.

BREAD OF LIFE, by Slaves of the Immaculate Heart of Mary, Still River, Mass.

GATE OF HEAVEN, by Slaves of the Immaculate Heart of Mary, Still River, Mass.

OUR GLORIOUS POPES, by Slaves of the Immaculate Heart of Mary, Still River, Mass.

SAINTS TO KNOW AND LOVE, by Slaves of the Immaculate Heart of Mary, Still River, Mass.

SAINTS TO REMEMBER, by Slaves of the Immaculate Heart of Mary, Still River, Mass.

THE COMMUNION OF SAINTS, by Slaves of the Immaculate Heart of Mary, Still River, Mass.

WHAT THE CATHOLIC CHURCH IS AND WHAT SHE TEACHES, by Fr. E. R. Hull, S.J.

THE BIBLE AN AUTHORITY ONLY IN CATHOLIC HANDS, by Our Sunday Visitor Press, Huntington, Indiana

THE TRUTH ABOUT CATHOLICS, by Fr. Joseph B. Ward

INDEX